CARDINAL JEAN-MARIE LUSTIGER
ON CHRISTIANS AND JEWS

Studies in
Judaism and Christianity

*Exploration of Issues in the
Contemporary Dialogue Between
Christians and Jews*

Editors
Lawrence Boadt, CSP
Kevin A. Lynch, CSP
Yehezkel Landau
Dr. Peter Pettit
Dr. Elena Procario-Foley
Dr. Ann Riggs
Michael Kerrigan, CSP

 A STIMULUS BOOK

CARDINAL JEAN-MARIE LUSTIGER ON CHRISTIANS AND JEWS

Edited by Jean Duchesne

A STIMULUS BOOK
PAULIST PRESS ✷ NEW YORK ✷ MAHWAH, NJ

Cover design by Lynn Else
Book design by Lynn Else and Theresa M. Sparacio

Library of Congress Cataloging-in-Publication Data

Lustiger, Jean-Marie, 1926–2007.
    [Selections. English. 2010]
    Cardinal Jean-Marie Lustiger on Christians and Jews / edited by Jean Duchesne.
       p. cm.
    "A Stimulus book."
    Includes bibliographical references (p.   ).
    ISBN 978-0-8091-4353-5 (alk. paper)
    1. Judaism—Relations—Christianity. 2. Christianity and other religions—Judaism. 3. Judaism—Relations—Catholic Church. 4. Catholic Church—Relations—Judaism. I. Duchesne, Jean. II. Title. III. Title: On Christians and Jews.
    BM535.L77 2010
    261.2´6—dc22
                                                                              2010009560

Published by Paulist Press
997 Macarthur Boulevard
Mahwah, New Jersey 07430

www.paulistpress.com

Printed and bound in the
United States of America

Contents

Introduction
Avery Cardinal Dulles, SJ

It is an honor to be asked to introduce the English translation of this book. Cardinal Jean-Marie Lustiger has been one of the most interesting and outstanding leaders of the Catholic Church in recent years. When he grew up in Paris as the son of Polish Jewish immigrants, hardly anyone could have foreseen his future as a man of the church. Yet there were signs of promise. By the age of twelve he had devoured the entire Bible in a Protestant version with passionate interest, and in 1940, at the age of fourteen, he requested and received baptism in the Catholic Church, notwithstanding the reluctance of his parents to give him permission. Shortly afterwards, his mother was taken to Auschwitz, where she perished. Many other members of the family were likewise executed by the Nazis at Polish concentration camps.

After his ordination in 1954, Father Lustiger carried on a very successful ministry as a chaplain at the University of Paris for fifteen years. Pope John Paul II appointed him bishop of Orleans in 1979, and fourteen months later, in January 1981, archbishop of Paris, a post he held until his resignation in 2005. He has been a cardinal since 1983.

The interviews and addresses in the present collection deal chiefly with Jewish-Christian relations. Theological in character as the cardinal's reflections are, they are also experiential. They reflect the living thought of a man who has grappled very personally with the questions on which he writes, since he himself was, and in a sense remains, a Jew. With his keen sense of the particular, he reflects on the stages by which he was led from Judaism to what he came to regard as the plenitude of Judaism in Christ the divine Messiah. As I followed the author's argument, I began to think that perhaps the faith of Judaism ought to be seen as a normal step toward coming to Christianity—normal not in a statistical but in a theological sense, since the faith of ancient Israel was God's way of preparing the world for the historical advent of its Savior.

Christianity, as Cardinal Lustiger explains, admits men and women of every nation—the "Gentiles"—into that privileged intimacy with God that was granted to the Jews under the Mosaic covenant. Under one aspect it is a universalization of the Mosaic covenant, permitting Gentile believers to be grafted onto the vital root of Judaism. In developing this position, Lustiger relies on the famous metaphor of the wild branches and the cultivated olive tree in St. Paul's Letter to the Romans.

Yet it is not enough to say, with Franz Rosenzweig, that Christianity is Judaism for pagans. Jesus not only universalized the Jewish covenant; he also raised it to a higher plane, giving his partners in the new covenant a share in his own divine life. Jesus invites his followers to participate consciously through faith in the life of the triune God.

Although the cardinal evidently believes that the Christian covenant surpasses the earlier covenants with Noah, Abraham, and Moses, he rejects the position known as supersessionism. Christianity is not a replacement for Judaism but a completion in which Judaism comes to its fruition.

Needless to say, Cardinal Lustiger deplores the anti-Semitism that still affects some Christians in spite of recent official documents, such as the Declaration *Nostra Aetate* of the Second Vatican Council. Modern anti-Semitism, he contends, is a new phenomenon, differing radically from the anti-Judaism of some church fathers and medieval theologians. Unlike anti-Judaism, anti-Semitism rests on atheistic presuppositions and is implicitly anti-Christian.

At its best, the cardinal recalls, the medieval settlement was neither anti-Semitic nor anti-Judaic. It embodied the three principles laid down by Pope Gregory the Great in 598: "No forced conversions of the Jews, no attacks on their synagogues or their celebrations, mutual cooperation in civilian life." Even this formula, however, falls short of the religious freedom favored by our author. He believes in a pluralist society in which Judaism and Christianity enjoy the right to make their full contribution to the global civilization in the making.

The present volume touches on many other vitally important questions for Jewish-Christian relations. What does it mean to be a Jew? Is the concept ethnic, religious, or political? Can a baptized Jew remain a Jew? Are all Jews obliged to become Christians, or can some fulfill their calling by fidelity to their own law? Who is to blame for the crucifixion of Jesus? What providential role is Judaism called to play in the "age of the nations" that began with Jesus Christ? Are Christians and Jews associated as fellow children of God even when they are religiously divided? Must Christians of Asia and Africa turn to the Jewish Scriptures as pertinent for their own religion?

Cardinal Lustiger deals with these and other questions with sincerity and tact. His observations in these essays and interviews, deeply grounded in the life experience of a distinguished churchman, have an authority surpassing that of the isolated academic scholar. But they also contribute to the progress of scholarship by offering learned insights and by raising questions that the cardinal leaves for further exploration and discussion.

Avery Cardinal Dulles, SJ
September 1, 2006

1
Well, If I Must

Interview by Y. Ben Porat (Y.B.P.) and D. Judkowski (D.J.) in the Israeli daily *Yedioth Ahronoth*, 6, 15, and 21 January 1982; originally published in French in *Le Débat*, no. 20, May 1982; and in English in *Dare to Believe: Addresses, Sermons, Interviews, 1981–1984*, by Jean-Marie Cardinal Lustiger, The Crossroad Publishing Company, 1986. Translated into English by Maurice Couve de Murville, Archbishop Emeritus of Birmingham, England.

Y.B.P.: I would like to ask you, first of all, what difference do you see existing today between the Jewish people and the people of Israel. Is there any difference between them, do you think?

Cardinal Lustiger: It is difficult for me to answer because those are theoretical questions. Even among Jews there are different ways of stating the relation between Israeli identity and the identity of the Jewish people. I cannot pretend to have a definitive view on that question. But I can express my personal feelings; I would say that they are not identical but that one is part of the other.

The notion of the Jewish people has many different aspects; it can mean a religious belonging or a historical one. For a Jew, the feeling of belonging to a people is both very powerful and very fluid. It has different degrees. Historically, if one is talking about present-day Jewish consciousness, I don't see how one can define belonging to the Jewish people (I am not saying belonging to "Judaism") without some reference to the State of Israel. And I do

1

not see how the State of Israel can be defined without including the wider notion of the Jewish people. I know that in saying that I am disassociating myself from certain points of view; for instance, there used to be a "Canaanite" tendency among Israeli intellectuals[1]; I do not know if it still exists.

Y.B.P.: Yes, it does.

At the opposite end of the scale, I know that there are Jews, both in Israel and in the Diaspora, who consider that they are not committed to the State of Israel. So there cannot be a clear-cut answer. But for me a link does exist.

Y.B.P.: So you would say that the State of Israel is not a state like other states.

I can quite see that other states, when faced with the particular country called Israel, entertain the same sort of relation with it they have with any other state. I can quite see that politicians in Israel, who are faced with political problems, deal with them in the way that other states do (or in the way that they ought to do if they were honest and respected their proper ends and ideals). But it is nonetheless a unique state. Its origins, its identity are not the same as those of any other country. It is the outcome of an extraordinary utopia that became a historic reality. That utopia was brought up to date by the dreams of the European nineteenth century, but it stretches back through several thousand years of community consciousness. I cannot think of any comparable case in the whole of history.

However, one must also say that Israel is a state like other states, and it is proper to say this, otherwise Israel would come to occupy a position that would be threatening for other nations. There is also the risk of imposing on Israel a false messianic consciousness; that would be morally perverse and politically disastrous. There have been examples of "messianic states" in history and they have all come to a very bad end. A state must be a state.

However, whenever one hears Jewish people saying, either in Israel or elsewhere, "We want to be a people like any other," one cannot help wondering whether this desire includes a hidden temptation. Is it not for a Jew a way of running away from his or her vocation? So there is a kind of inner contradiction here. I expect you recognize the allusion to the first Book of Samuel, where that contradiction already exists.[2]

Y.B.P.: I would like to ask the question at a practical level, a personal level, almost. You have in front of you two Israeli journalists who are also Jews. Do you make the distinction? Do you think of us as Jews or do you think of us as Israelis, that is, two non-Frenchmen who hold the passports of a foreign state?

I find the distinction hard to make. But I can say this. I have often been to the Near East and to Israel; in fact, I have been there nearly every year since 1950, as a student first, then as a chaplain to students. Well, it seems to me that Israelis are not Jews like other Jews.

Y.B.P.: Is that a good thing or a bad thing?

I don't know. But I can quote two conversations I had sometime between 1950 and 1960. I met a Belgian Jew; he had been a doctor and became a teacher in a kibbutz, somewhere in Galilee. He had lost his entire family during the war so that he was alone in the world, and he made his *alyah*[3] to Israel. As there were too many doctors, he became a teacher. He was telling me that he liked the *sabras*.[4] But suddenly he said, "They no longer have that Jewish intelligence; they are slow, calm, pleasant" (laughter). He was a very cultured man and that was a most extraordinary thing to say.

At about the same time, I had a heated discussion, lasting all night, with the director of the school of agriculture in Galilee; you know, that round building. I think Moshe Dayan was a student there for a time.

Y.B.P.: Ygal Allon went there.

Did he? Anyway, the director I am talking about was an extraordinary person, an old man of Russian origin. I had shared some of my misgivings with him. I said: "You are creating here a national consciousness. That's a good thing. I can quite see the negative side of things for Jews in Europe, and it is in reaction to it that you exist here. You are developing a utopia; only here, it has become a reality. You and your contemporaries are rooted in the consciousness of a particular historical situation. But what about the generation that will come after you? Where will its strength come from? Will nationalism alone suffice to provide the will to survive? What will the inner coherence of the people be? How will people be motivated for sacrifice? This drive to become "people like other peoples," does it not come finally from the fact that you were not like other people? When the day comes that you are just like other nations, when you are just Israelites, from where will the will come to live differently from other nations? And what will your contact be, then, with the Jews throughout the world?

Y.B.P.: That's exactly the question I am asking you. But how do you see the Jews? Do you see them as having special attributes?

What do you mean by that?

D.J.: Are they considered particularly intelligent?

I shouldn't rely on that judgment, as it is made by non-Jews (laughter). I would tend to give a theological definition of what a Jew is; that is, a religious definition.

Y.B.P.: Go ahead.

It is given in the Bible: "a gathering of individuals whom God has made into a people." God made them into a people of his gift, and it was not for their sake but for the sake of the whole world. Now, one has to ask: "What was the effect of this calling on the historical consciousness of the Jewish people?" For a culture was born as well, and that culture is not irrelevant to Jewish consciousness. It is part of the commandment that is: to transmit the commandments to one's children and to guarantee the future by means of one's children. Here you have both the promise and the commandments. It is not by accident, therefore, that Judaism has survived. It continues through history, brings forth its own culture, and creates an attitude and a way of existing that are unique. That, too, belongs to its essence. The Jewish people is conscious of its past in history and it knows that it has a future for which it is responsible, not just for itself but by reason of the gift that it received at the beginning. That is where you find the basis for the Jewish people's attitude to history; it is an attitude that enabled it during several thousand years to cope with existence in Diaspora, and that was long before the coming of Christianity. That, surely, is something quite unique.

There's nothing like it in history. I know there are gypsies, but they are migrants, and it is not as migrants that the Jews have maintained their unique character throughout the centuries.

Y.B.P.: What about the idea of being a "chosen people"? Is that an idea that Christians can accept? Do Christians still think of the Jews as the chosen people? Do you?

I think that it's a key idea for the understanding of faith. If you don't have that concept, you cannot understand either Judaism or Christianity. But if you leave the area of faith and secularize the concept, you end up with things like the German army having *Gott Mit Uns* on their belts. It becomes intolerable.

D.J.: Do you agree with General de Gaulle's comment on the Jews: "An elite people, self-assured and dominating"? Was he right?

At the time, I thought it a humorous expression, because the picture of the Jew projected by the period I had witnessed was one of the Jew persecuted and done to death. And here he was calling the Jews "an elite people." I don't mind if that's the new image people have of the Jews (laughter); anyway, it blotted out a caricature that had lasted for many centuries. But it's also true that General de Gaulle spoke with a certain touch of grandeur, not necessarily pejorative coming from him. That is what was remembered of his witticism, and no doubt he meant it to be so understood.

D.J.: Do you think he was anti-Semitic, perhaps unconsciously?

No, I don't think so. I think that by upbringing, De Gaulle belonged to that section of conservatives who are both republican and socially conscious. It is only after his time that anti-Semitism tried to come to the fore in France. It could not do so in De Gaulle's time.

Y.B.P.: Your Excellency, there is a question that everyone in Israel is asking since you became archbishop of Paris and appeared on Israeli TV, where what you said was much appreciated. The question is: What do you think is the difference between Judaism and Christianity? I know that it's a rather complex question.

It's very complex.

Y.B.P.: But I've come all the way to Paris especially to ask it!

In order to answer, I have to overcome a great difficulty, which is that I am not speaking to you two only, but to all your readers as well, and I don't know where they stand. All sorts of misunderstandings are possible. I respect Jewish people; I am very conscious of the indignation they might feel toward my personal position and of the feelings of opposition they might have; so in trying to answer, I might be hurting their legitimate feelings. I do know what some people think of a Jew who becomes a Christian. I don't want to be provocative and I don't want to offend anybody, so it has always been with very great reluctance that I have given any personal explanations.

There is a preliminary point I would like to make. I have claimed to be a Jew, but that was not at all in order to enter into a theological debate. I never claimed to be at the same time a good Jew according to the requirements of the rabbis and a good Christian according to the requirements of the church. But I am sure you understand that I cannot repudiate my Jewish condition without losing my own dignity and the respect I owe to my parents and to all those to whom I belong; that is true both in times of persecution and in times of peace. I claim to be a Jew not to hurt anyone, but because I respect the truth and what is due to the truth.

I knew when I claimed to be a Jew that a certain number of misunderstandings would occur and that I would not be understood. When I say that I acted out of respect for the dignity of being a Jew and for my own self-respect, I meant that I could not cease to be Jewish. Obviously I am not an observant Jew in the sense understood by those who define Jewish orthodoxy. But what I can say is that in becoming a Christian, I did not intend to cease being the Jew I was then. I was not running away from the Jewish condition. I have that from my parents, and I can never lose it. I have it from God, and he will never let me lose it.

Y.B.P.: But surely you were prepared to move on to something else, even if you did have a deep respect for the Jews.

That's right.

Y.B.P.: Doesn't that mean that you thought that something else was more correct, better, more divine—I don't know how to put it.

Yes, my way of putting it was: a better way of being Jewish, according to what I knew then of Judaism.

Y.B.P.: But you did move on from one condition to another, and you chose the latter.

That's true; but I did not move on from being Jewish to "not being Jewish." That would have been impossible.

Y.B.P.: Didn't you move on to another religion because you thought it true?

Yes, but as if carried in the womb of the first one.

Y.B.P.: Can I ask you some personal questions, I hope you won't mind? Did you become a Christian at fourteen?

Yes.

D.J.: Do you remember how it happened? Was it the result of a revelation or of evolution? Do you remember how you felt at the time?

Up till now I have always felt slightly embarrassed about answering questions like that. I hate exhibitionism. But of course if one says nothing, people imagine all sorts of things. There was another reason for not saying too much, which was that parents could have been blamed. People could have said: "They were a bad lot. If they had given their children a Jewish education, things would not have turned out as they did." I know there must be some people who think that way. Anyhow, since you have asked the question, I will try to answer.

When I was a child, I was conscious of being Jewish in exactly the same ways as any son of Jewish immigrants in France. There was nothing special about me. I wasn't called Durand or Dupont; my first name is Aron [Cardinal Lustiger insisted that his first name be spelled "Aron," not "Aaron"—Jean Duchesne], after my paternal grandfather. I was called Aron at school. My mother had come to France as a child. My father came at eighteen and never spoke perfect French. We were hard up; I wasn't dressed as well as the other children, but I was fairly often first in my class, and that was another thing that made me different from the others. At the entrance to the Lycée Montaigne, I had my face bashed in because I was Jewish. Sometimes when I came up to a group of boys who were talking, they would say, "Push off, you filthy Jew." I know about all that. I also knew that being Jewish was something special. My parents were not believers; I still remember some of the things they used to say: "Rabbis, priests, they all talk the same rubbish...." But I had the sense of the presence of God; I remember that very well. Very little is needed to awaken the sense of God's presence in the mind of a child. What I remember is the way my mother used to say the blessing over the first fruits. That was all. It was enough for me. And then, aged ten, I secretly read through the whole of the Bible.

D.J.: What, at ten years old?

Yes, I was supposed to be practicing the piano or doing my homework. My parents were down in the shop, and they couldn't see what I was up to.

D.J.: Was this before the war?

It must have been 1936 or 1937. My parents had a bookcase that was locked, and I was not supposed to read any of the books in it. It contained all sorts of books my parents had bought. They had a great respect for books and bought more or less anything. The key was kept on top of the bookcase, so it wasn't very difficult for me to stand on a chair and find it. I opened the bookcase and read all sorts of things. I read Zola; I read Abel Hermant. I read all those boring novels that came out between the wars; you know, a series brought out by Flammarion and bound in green. But I also found the Bible, a Protestant Bible, and I read it right through.

D.J.: The Old Testament?

The Old and the New Testaments. I read the Bible passionately and I didn't say a word to anybody. I cannot remember whether I was eleven or twelve at the time, but from then onward I began to think about these things and to mull them over. I always went to public school and not to a Catholic school. My teachers were completely neutral in matters of religion. When I was eleven, I had a Latin teacher who was Jewish, but I only found out after the war. I also remember the history lessons when I was eleven. When we were taught about the Hebrews in class, I thought it wasn't much compared to what I already knew. Literature too was important; it influenced me and started me thinking. I can remember, too, a holiday at Berck when I was thirteen.[5] I was only a child, but I was faced then with the suffering of other children, the problem of something obviously evil, the problem of death. I seemed to receive in my understanding an absolute confirmation of the existence of God, God who is the only just one in contrast to the injustice done to human beings.

But before that, I had come across Nazism in real life. For two years running, when I was eleven and twelve, my parents sent me off to Germany for a month during the summer all on my own, to stay with a family and learn German. I don't know whether they realized what they were doing or whether they were just daring. I had my real name on my father's passport. The families were anti-Nazi, but the second year I stayed with a family of teachers, and their children, who were a little older than me, were in the Hitler Youth, which was compulsory. So at the age of eleven I saw Nazism as it really is. Can you imagine what it meant to a boy of eleven to be talking things over with a lad of thirteen who was in the Hitler Youth? He showed me his knife and said, "At the summer solstice we are going to kill all the Jews." I heard that with my own ears. I read the anti-Semitic placards that the Blackshirts put up in the streets. I knew Hitler for what he was; I wasn't at all surprised by the way Nazism turned out, subsequently.

By 1937 everything was perfectly clear for that particular French Jewish boy of eleven who had had the opportunity of talking with German boys of twelve or thirteen. I could see what other French Jews, adults, could not yet see, perhaps. Perhaps German Jews could not see it either. So you see, I was deeply marked by all this; nothing of what happened later surprised me. What I mean is that I could not be surprised by what I had understood outright and intuitively as a child.

It was in Germany, too, that I first met adults who were Christians, and I was impressed by the fact that they were anti-Nazi; that was the one thing that struck me about them. It was in Germany, too, that I guessed why God has committed himself to the Jews because of the Messiah. It is the opposite of *Gott Mit Uns* on soldiers' belts.

So it was in those years that I began to draw near to Christianity, by thinking, by reading. Those were the only influences on me, books and the culture I was imbibing at the lycée from different teachers. Later on I found out about the beliefs of those teachers; some were Jewish, some were committed Catholics, some were unbelievers, others were agnostics. But I had a long interior path to follow and, fundamentally, it was Christ who gave me the key to my searchings, Christ as Messiah and image of the Jewish people. At the same time, I knew that persecution had been the lot of the Jews in history and that it had also been the source of their dignity.

At the time, I wanted to become a doctor, because I thought that was the best way of helping humankind. My parents had taught me that, if people thought of us as different, we ought to be better than others, more just, serving all, defending the poor and the unfortunate. I couldn't see any better way of serving humankind than being a doctor. That's what I thought at the time, or else I might have wanted to become a great writer like Zola so as to defend the oppressed.

D.J.: But you said you were influenced by the Bible.

I was.

D.J.: Were you shocked by anything you read in the Bible? What happened exactly?

I cannot remember. I found everything in the Bible surprising but nothing shocking.

D.J.: Did you share your thoughts with your parents?

No, not at all.

Y.B.P.: So it was a real conversion?

It was more like a crystallization than a conversion. Through the circumstances I have mentioned, I found that, when I first really confronted Christians, I knew their beliefs better than they did themselves. When I reread the Gospels at that stage, I already knew them. I say "at that stage" because it was then that my parents absolutely refused to accept that I was convinced; they thought it was disgusting. I said to them, "I am not leaving you. I'm not going over to the enemy. I am becoming what I am. I am not ceasing to be a Jew; on the contrary, I am discovering another way of being a Jew." I know that Jewish people think that's a scandalous way to talk, but that's what I experienced. When I chose my Christian names, I chose three Jewish names: Aron-Jean-Marie. It's obvious if you look at the Hebrew forms. I kept the name I had received at birth.

D.J.: Earlier on you spoke of the way the values of Judaism persisted in Christianity. Now you are saying, "I discovered the values of Judaism in becoming a Christian." What exactly do you mean? What values are you talking about?

I mean God's calling of a people, so that they could know him, love him, and serve him. I mean the promise of universal salvation, prepared for all men and women. I mean the joy of being with God and of being loved by him. I mean the understanding of the history of Israel as the history of salvation, as opposed to the history of damnation that the war was displaying at the time. I also mean the value of that historical belonging that is not just due to chance but is the unfolding of the love of God, our love for God, and God's love for us.

Y.B.P.: I believe that you became a Catholic at Orleans when you were fourteen.

At Orleans, that's right.

Y.B.P.: Did you decide to become a minister then?

Yes, I did.

Y.B.P.: Right at the start, then, you knew that you would become a priest?

Yes, for me it was clear right from the start. But I didn't mention it to anybody.

Y.B.P.: Was it the same idea of service that you'd had previously when you decided to become a doctor?

Yes, it was.

Y.B.P.: But couldn't you have served humankind from within Judaism?

For me at the time, the contents of Judaism were no different from what I was discovering in Christianity. I saw Judaism then as a historical condition marked by persecution; I did not think for one moment of leaving it. But it found its fulfillment in welcoming the person of Jesus, the Messiah of Israel; it was in recognizing him, and only in recognizing him, that Judaism found its meaning.

Y.B.P.: Did you see the persecution of Israel as a punishment?
No, I did not.
Y.B.P.: Didn't you accept the view that God had punished the Jewish people because it did not recognize Jesus?
No, I never thought that way at all.
Y.B.P.: I think I told you that I was hidden by a priest during the war. I shan't tell you his name, as he is probably still alive. I used to serve his Mass during the three months I was there; it was in the south of France. I was fifteen at the time; I was in hiding at his house and he saved the life of many children. He never tried to convert us, not at all, but what he tried to get across was: "You see, my child, you are being persecuted because your people did not recognize the Messiah." Isn't that Christian doctrine?
That sort of thing has been said. It was one of the ways of understanding the fate of Israel in Christian countries. But I never accepted that view.
Y.B.P.: Don't you think the Vatican will be after you for having said that in an interview?
Saying what?
Y.B.P.: Saying that phrase, "the Jews are persecuted because they refuse to acknowledge Jesus," is not a sort of creed.
No, I don't think it will, because that statement is not part of Catholic faith.
Y.B.P.: So if a priest said that sort of thing to me, it was his personal interpretation?
It was his personal interpretation. It is an interpretation that is quite widely diffused and accepted, but it is not part of faith. So in telling you that I do not accept such a view, I cannot be suspected of professing a deviationist opinion.
Y.B.P.: But isn't what you are saying going against common opinion?
What I am saying will no doubt surprise those people who go no deeper than generally accepted ideas and prejudices. That is because Christian thinking on the destiny of Israel, on the Jewish condition, and on the place of Judaism in the history of salvation is only just beginning to emerge in modern times.

Y.B.P.: But surely you ought to be saving us: "Look here, if you want to be good Jews, if you really want to be saved, you should become Christians." And yet you aren't saying it, and I am not trying to get you to say it. But I do think it would be logical if you did.

Not necessarily, and for this reason: it is not up to us to decide what we should be. It is up to God. It is up to God to decide who I must be and what I must do; God decides first and I decide afterward.

But there is another, deeper side to your question that I want to look at with great fear and trepidation, and then I will come back to the question as you formulated it. What is the meaning of being Jewish today? How should one be a Jew so as to be faithful to Judaism? The answer isn't as obvious as all that. Similarly, it isn't obvious exactly what being a Christian means, and there are different ways of being a Christian.

I think that the situation of Jews in the Diaspora today is very different from what it was before the destruction of the temple. Judaism has had a unique spiritual experience. During those two thousand years, the unique phenomenon called rabbinism has occurred. As a result, something of great value was safeguarded, which is Jewish identity; but in order to achieve this, the rabbis had to choose between various options. As a result, there were many aspirations that were disregarded by the official majority; many questions and many trends within Judaism were not identified or recognized.

Moreover, new problems have arisen since the beginning of modern times, since the eighteenth century and the beginnings of emancipation. The problem of Jewish identity does not only concern Jewish identity from the legal point of view; it is a problem of Jewish fidelity. That seems to me a very important question. It has a bearing on the question that you have raised, because historically the controversy between Judaism and Christianity has had two sides to it. There is the aspect that concerns the way in which Judaism relates to its own claims and to its own traditions. There is also the way in which Christians, or shall we say groups within a

Christian culture, identify and recognize the specific Jewish heritage, with its richness and diversity, as they exist today.

In modern Christian theology, the relation between Judaism and Christianity has hardly been tackled. All the elements of the problem are there; they call out for a fundamental examination, but for historical reasons these questions have been put to one side and passed over. This is especially true of the questions concerning the origins of Christianity, its relation to Judaism, and the way in which Judaism reacted toward it. When the New Testament was written, the lines were already partly drawn up, but only partly so. Afterward, the differences became more serious. The first problem is to understand the relation between Israel and the nations. That's a vital point; the revelation made to Israel is also for the nations. In the tradition, we find a series of covenants, the covenant with Noah, and so on.[6] One has to ask: "Was the covenant with Noah the only kind of covenant that was offered to the nations? Were there not other possibilities in the prophets? The covenant with Noah already implies a great deal; in fact, since it involves moral rectitude, it already implies everything. But were not the Gentiles called to receive something from Judaism itself? Does not the Bible itself announce something more than the covenant of Noah when it proclaims the promise made to Abraham and the revelation on Mount Sinai?"

Y.B.P.: Yes, other answers may be found in the tradition.

So you agree that other answers may be found. Well, that was precisely the cause of the crisis that occurred from 70 to 140 during the first century of Christianity. The question was whether pagans, people coming from the *goyim*,[7] could enter into the covenant. And one also has to ask to what extent were some of the promises fulfilled at that time and which ones they were. When the messianic titles were applied to Jesus, what happened to the image of the Messiah as far as Jews were concerned? And what image of the Messiah did Christians accept, then and now? These are the questions that Christians and Jews inevitably put to each other.

Most of the Christians, when they entered into the covenant, were pagans in origin, but they forgot that they were born into paganism. As you know, the word *church* translates the Hebrew word *qahal*.[8]

Y.B.P.: That's why the Book of Ecclesiastes is Qoheleth in Hebrew.

Exactly. So the church is a gathering together that is summoned by God.

Y.B.P.: Right.

When we talk about the *Catholic* Church, we are using a word derived from the Greek *kath' holon* (according to the whole), which means according to the totality of Jews and Gentiles. That's different from talking about the universal church, meaning only the totality of the nations. Yet you often find it translated that way. For example, ill-translating the creed, Protestants substitute the word *universal* for *Catholic*; universality would then be a horizontal notion, like the United Nations.

Y.B.P.: Quite.

But the Greek phrase *kath' holon* really means the *qahal*, composed of Jews who have been the object of God's choice. So that "totality" of humanity according to God's plan is made up of Israel and the nations, who are to be finally united in the one and only covenant. If you put things that way, it is clear that the last days have not yet been fulfilled.

You might say, "But where can you see the promises of the Messiah actually fulfilled?" That is the real question between us. In a way, they haven't been fulfilled. History continues; its present condition is that the fulfillment remains hidden. That is the Christian belief. The figure of the Messiah is a hidden one. Christians tend to forget sometimes that they are still waiting for the coming in glory of their Messiah.

Israel, on the other hand, must remain faithful as long as the times are not accomplished; it is still loved by God because of his election and because of the patriarchs. God's gifts and his call cannot be abolished. It is obviously a very difficult question because, from the Jewish point of view, Christianity has anticipated things and is in too much of a hurry. And that's true too; Judaism retains a valid point of view on Christianity; what it says is relevant.

What one cannot say, as the Marxists do, is that Christianity has sought refuge in spiritual things and in the next life. On the contrary, Christianity is very realistic in its outlook. But this is an area where one has to challenge a good many prejudices and assumptions; if I were to go into it fully, I would need more columns than your paper is prepared to give me.

Y.B.P.: So what you are saying is that Christianity is a sort of "open" Judaism, a Judaism that has been opened to the world and to the pagans. Christianity consists in making the Gentiles participate in Judaism. It is this achievement that has given us Christianity.

Yes, in a way, but in a way that was unexpected both for Israel and for the pagans.

Y.B.P.: And were the pagans told, "You can now join in"?

Yes, that is what the first Christian community of Jerusalem, which was composed exclusively of those who were Jewish by birth, eventually came around to accepting, after much controversy. The person of Jesus, once he was recognized as Messiah, brought into focus a whole range of Jewish expectations that were seen to have a special spiritual content and that were experienced, at that moment, as fulfilled in the Christian experience.

D.J.: So, if you can remember what you thought as a child, you considered Jesus the Christ as a Jewish Messiah?

Yes.

D.J.: And do you still think of him that way?

Most certainly I do, and I am not alone in this. The Christian Scriptures say that Jesus is the Jewish Messiah. It is only translation that obscures the fact that Jesus Christ means Jesus the Messiah.

Y.B.P.: So, if I understand you, you are saying something like this: on the one hand, it is right to be a Christian but, on the other hand, it is right to remain a Jew because we need the Jews precisely as Jews.

Yes, according to what God decides.

Y.B.P.: So that this view of the future may be fulfilled?

Yes. You are leading me on to theological and spiritual questions.

Y.B.P.: But isn't that what we are talking about?

All right, but then you have to accept certain presuppositions, otherwise the dialogue takes on a certain wild and extravagant quality. That is why I am being cautious. We are in that period of history in which God is fulfilling the promise made to Israel "until the fullness of time is achieved." The Church, too, is grappling with a historical question. In the early church, the church of the first two centuries, there was a "Church of Jerusalem," that is, a Christian church composed of Jews. It was the same throughout the Roman Empire. One of the constant problems of the early Church was the coexistence of Jewish Christians and Gentile Christians within the new Church, the new *qahal*, the *qahal* of the Messiah. The great difficulty, where this coexistence was concerned, was provided by the ritual laws. Were the Gentile converts to Christianity bound to keep all the prescriptions of Judaism? Should they be circumcised? Did they have to keep the dietary laws? What obligations were they taking on? Those were the questions that Christians were asking about Gentile converts, just as Jews were asking them about their proselytes. But they were not rejecting Judaism as such.

Y.B.P.: This respect that you have for Judaism and for Jews, doesn't it come from the fact that you are a Jew yourself and that your name is Aron? After all, lots of other Christians don't speak with such respect for Judaism, nor do many priests and church people.

That may be so, but it's so much the worse for them. It is a pity that Christians, who nearly all are from a Gentile origin, should have kept a Gentile mentality. Jesus never claimed to be "king of the Jews"; that title was given to him by a pagan, the Roman Pilate. At the time, the Jews in Israel did not refer to themselves as "Jews"; they used the expression "the people of Israel." It was outsiders who called them Jews. The Gospel of Matthew, which was composed in a Jewish milieu, is very precise in its terminology in this respect.

If Christians were faithful to the gift that God has made to them, they would understand that God has made them "children of

God," "sons of God," as are the children of Israel, but in a different way; they would see that this gift takes place in the person of the Messiah who welcomes them; they would understand that they have benefited in a superabundant way from the gift made in the first place to Israel, although Israel itself does not always realize the full greatness of that gift. My deepest desire is that there should be on both sides gratitude and mutual recognition. I wish that Christians would not forget that they have been grafted on to the one and only stock of Israel; and that stock lives on. I am commenting on the words of Paul, of course.[9]

Y.B.P.: It's a metaphor.

That's right, and it's an unusual one because he says that the wild olive shoot had been grafted onto a cultivated olive. But in fact a gardener does the opposite; it is the stock that is wild and it is the graft that is taken from the cultivated plant. Whereas what Paul does in describing the relation between Gentile Christians and Jews is to say, "You, the pagans, are the wild shoot and you are grafted on to the cultivated olive root, the Jews"; and he adds, "and you have become the branches of the tree according to your nature."

There's another aspect that gives great hope, I think. Thanks to the spiritual and cultural freedom that Israeli nationhood has brought about and thanks to a different outlook on the part of Christians, it is now possible, perhaps, for Judaism to recognize Christianity as an offspring of God. After all, could Judaism, while remaining faithful to its call from God, recognize one day that the nations that have become Christian are also like unexpected children for the Jewish people? It would be like the gift of an unexpected offspring who has not yet been recognized as such. Since Christians have not acknowledged that the Jews are as their older brothers, and the stock on which they have been grafted, perhaps the Jews themselves could recognize the pagan nations that have become Christian as their younger brother. But there has to be forgiveness first because of all the persecutions, all the fratricidal conflict. Precisely because they are so alike, there has been a kind of war of legitimation. It is the old story of wanting to kill one's brother so as to have the whole inheritance. The reason for persecution has been jealousy, in the spiritual sense; but jealousy could become emulation and so become a source of blessings.

Y.B.P.: Have you studied Judaism?

I have done some reading out of interest, but I have not been through a course of Talmudic studies in the proper sense. That needs excessive specialization; but I have read quite a lot.

Y.B.P.: Have you learned Hebrew?

Hardly. I can read biblical Hebrew, but I have not learned modern Hebrew. I started, then I had to give up.

D.J.: Have you been aware of any prejudice against you because of your Jewish antecedents?

You mean from Christians?

D.J.: Yes, from Christians, and from your colleagues.

It's hard to say, because I do not worry much about what people are thinking about me. I think it's unhealthy to be always wondering what effect one is having. I would be furious if there were an opinion poll to find out what people think about me because of my Jewish origins. That would seem to me to be an indiscreet question and an unhealthy one. But of course there may be pockets of anti-Semitism here and there; it could hardly be otherwise. It is also possible that in a period of emergency, I might become a target and a scapegoat. But one thing I do notice: I stand for a good deal more than what I am as an individual. It is not only I as an individual who matter, but everything I stand for historically. I can see that the decision that gave me such a notable responsibility has been for many Christians a reminder of that historical and spiritual reality that I have called "the roots." It is like a living reminder of their past history that they have often been tempted to forget.

I am alluding here to a problem that is peculiar to Christians. After all, it is because of Judaism that Christianity recognizes Jesus as Messiah, the son of God, meaning by that what the Bible means by calling him Messiah-king and also eternal Wisdom. It is only because of certain criteria, inherited from Judaism, that Christianity is preserved from the temptation of appropriating Jesus as a mythological character and adapting him to all circumstances, and to every culture. Such is the criterion that has allowed Christian faith to preserve its true and authentic character. There has always been a tendency, which is particularly strong today, to accept Christ as a divine personage and to deck him out with whatever qualities a particular culture is endowed with. But it is the Bible that tells us the real nature of God's choice, and that is what makes it impossible to identify Christ and Apollo or Dionysus. Judaism is the witness of that unique choice. For Christians, it is the Jews who are the living witnesses of the unique and historical character of Christian faith.

It is impossible to understand anything about Christian belief if one does not accept God's choice of a Messiah, and one cannot understand God's choice of a Messiah if one does not accept his choice of Israel. It is when people want to do away with this foundation of Christianity that they start persecuting Jews and wanting to blot them out. The history of Christianity shows us an example of this negative attitude toward Judaism that has been condemned by the church; I am alluding to the heresy of Marcion, who wanted to produce a version of the Gospels without any allusions to the Old Testament. Although this view was condemned by the Church as heretical, it turns up again in modern times. You know that certain Protestant German historians argued from the fact that Jesus was a Galilean, and therefore he must have been an Aryan.

There can be a similar temptation for Western Christians when they present Christianity to African and Asian peoples; they are tempted to pass over Jesus' Jewish nature. They say, "The Gospel is a way of life." So there is a risk that when Africans become Christians, they may say, "Our African culture takes the place of the Old Testament as far as we, African Christians, are concerned." And Asians might say, "The sacred writings of Asia are the Old Testament for us." Are they right or wrong? Where does the Christian religion find its balance? During the synod of bishops in Rome in 1974, Cardinal Marty emphatically recalled the obligation of accepting the whole of Scripture; one cannot jettison the Old Testament under the pretext of being faithful to the New Testament in its confrontation with pagan culture, its "inculturation," as we call it.

Y.B.P.: Because the Ten Commandments are in the Old Testament, after all.

Yes. The Ten Commandments and their twofold summary that are traditional in Judaism: "Listen, O Israel, you shall love the Lord your God" (Deut 6:4–5) and "You will love your neighbor as yourself" (Lev 19:18); these are central to the prayer and to the teaching of Jesus and to the faithfulness of Christianity (Luke 10:25–8). It is not an accident that the whole of Christianity's understanding of humanity refers back explicitly and insistently to the beginning of the Torah, the first chapters of Genesis; this has been brought out especially by John Paul II.

One must admit that there is a real danger of altering the Christian faith from the inside and making it into a form of paganism. Many periods and cultures have been tempted to submerge Christianity into a form of paganism. It is true that Christianity has to live out a certain tension from the very fact that it is called to be a "light for the nations." But in the present state of things, it can only be true to itself if it continues to receive the gift that was made to Israel. However, there was a twofold break in the past; it occurred when the Jewish authorities said, "One cannot be faithful to the synagogue if one is a disciple of Jesus"; and the Christians said, "One cannot be a Christian if one belongs institutionally to Judaism." There was a deep break, a parting of the waters.

Y.B.P.: So one could suppose, as one listens to you (perhaps you cannot say this but I can say it for you), that you feel in part more Jewish than not.

I don't know. I certainly do feel very much a Jew.

Y.B.P.: If one moves away from the spiritual and religious aspect, can you say that you feel solidarity with Jews throughout the world? What are your feelings when you read newspaper reports about Jews being persecuted in Soviet Russia because they are Jews?

How can one not feel solidarity with father, mother, or cousins if they are ill or persecuted? You cannot possibly expect that I would answer your question in any other way. They are my brothers.

D.J.: Would it be very indiscreet if we were to ask you to tell us about the main stages of your life? You have told us what hap-

*pened when you were fourteen, but what happened afterwards, in
1940 and 1942?*

I do hate talking about myself in public.

D.J.: I know, but it's a very understanding public.

No, really; I don't feel...

D.J.: And it's a public that is very well disposed toward you.

I am sure of that; but everything one says gets around. It
always does.

D.J.: Not necessarily.

Y.B.P.: Since we publish in Hebrew.

Well, if I must, I must. I will try to share some of my memories. It was wartime. I had to flee from the town I was living in and
to hide, otherwise I would have been betrayed. There were precise
threats to that effect, and I had been warned about them. One had
to register with the police; at first my parents hadn't registered, and
then in the end they did.

D.J.: Was this at Orleans?

Yes, but my parents had stayed in Paris. In 1940 they had
given me permission to be baptized, but inwardly they did not agree
at all. I had asked for it repeatedly and they gave in. Perhaps they
thought it might afford some protection against the persecution that
was already threatening in the summer of 1940. But for me it had a
quite different meaning. Then it became obligatory for Jews to
wear the star of David. We tried everything, false papers, and so on.
Anyway, I won't go into details. My father went off to the unoccu-
pied zone of France to go into hiding and prepare the way. My
mother stayed behind to mind the shop and maintain some sort of
livelihood; food was short. Then she was arrested. First, the shop
was put under the "oversight" of an "Aryan" administrator, like all
Jewish shops. Then it was confiscated. The flat was pillaged and
then occupied by "Aryans." My mother was arrested because she
had been reported for not wearing the yellow star. She was interned
at Drancy.[10] We tried every possible way of getting her out. Then
she was taken away and finally deported. Later I learned that she
had gone to Auschwitz when I read the memorial of French Jews
edited by S. Klarsfeld. At the time we had no news of any sort. But

she knew that all the Jews were going to be killed; people knew it at Drancy. She told us so in a letter that had been smuggled out of Drancy by the guards, in return for cash. I had left Orleans and was in a boarding school, where I finished my secondary education and got my baccalaureate. I crossed secretly into the nonoccupied zone and joined up with my father. For a year I worked in a factory, and I also started studying for a degree in chemistry. I took part in underground movements; I used to distribute copies of *Témoignage chrétien*. It was no more than what numerous young people of seventeen and eighteen were doing in France at the time. Then came the Liberation. I wanted to be a priest; it was my own idea. My father was utterly opposed. So for two years I read for a degree in literature. I took part in the work of the student union.

D.J.: Was that in Paris?

Yes. Then in 1946 I entered the university seminary, the Séminaire des Carmes at the Institut Catholique in Paris, and in 1954 I was ordained a priest. I was student chaplain until 1969. My responsibility was the chaplaincy at the Sorbonne and other universities in Paris. I met a lot of people in the intellectual world of Paris at the time. Then for ten years I was parish priest of a place on the edge of Paris, near Boulogne. And then, to my great surprise, I was appointed bishop of Orleans by the pope; but I was even more surprised when I was appointed archbishop of Paris. So there you are.

D.J.: How do they make these decisions? Do you know the process by which you were chosen as archbishop of Paris? Did you know the pope personally?

No, I only met him after I became a bishop. The decision was his. The nuncio submits a certain number of names and says, "These are the people one is thinking of," and he finds out about the candidates.

Y.B.P.: So he must have said that this one was originally Jewish?

He must have.

D.J.: Do you think that's why you were chosen?

I don't know. How could I?

D.J.: Haven't you ever talked about it with the pope?

No, never. But when I had been appointed, I wrote to him telling him that my parents came from Bendzyn and that most of my family had been killed at Auschwitz or elsewhere in Poland. He had known all about it when he decided to appoint me.

Y.B.P.: That really is very important for us.

Quite.

Y.B.P.: What is an archbishop supposed to do? We don't know.

If only I knew! I seem to be caught up with hundreds of problems. I have to help the Christians who live in Paris to live in the Christian faith and to live up to their Christian faith. There are other sides to it as well. Since France is very centralized and Paris is preponderant, the archbishop of Paris is, in a way, an official person. He is in contact with all sorts of people; that's the best known side of my work, so I mention it first so as not to forget it. The ambassadors of foreign countries announced that they wanted to pay courtesy calls; I haven't accepted yet, as I just haven't got the time. If I were not careful, all my time would go on official functions. Many I cannot get out of. For instance, every foreign bishop passing through Paris wants to pay a courtesy call, and so on. It's due to the importance of Paris in today's world. Then there is all the work that has to be done by the French bishops, and sometimes by all the bishops of the world, because decisions have to be made. Our discussions are very democratic, in spite of what people might think. I know a lot of people think the church operates like the central committee of the Communist party (laughter).

Y.B.P.: Do you have a large administration?

No, it's small and not really adequate. But may I come back to what I consider to be my main task? I have to be faithful to the mission of priests and a man of God in relation to all the people I meet. I meet mostly people who are believers, but some unbelievers also. I have to help communities, parishes, movements, and groups to live their faith, to live the Christian life. The faithful are facing very difficult problems because of the rapid changes that have occurred in the way people behave, in living conditions, and in the place of the Church in modern society. There have been enormous changes over the last ten years or so. It would be very easy to become confined to an official role. Everything tends in that direction, especially the way we do things in France. I don't want it to be, but it's an uphill struggle.

Y.B.P.: Do you have time for meditation?

I make time.

Y.B.P.: Do you manage to get into your timetable: no interviews between such and such a time?

Yes, that's it. It's the only way to do it. Each week I have a whole day off, and each day I take at least an hour, over and above the recitation of the Divine Office. That's all the freedom I get.

Y.B.P.: Would you allow me to ask: Does an archbishop read nonreligious books? Do you go to the cinema? Do you watch television and read France Soir?

When I was a parish priest, I considered that it was my duty to devote about one-third of my time to personal study, reading, and reflection. Now that I have been catapulted into the responsibilities of an archbishop, I spend all my time dealing with emergencies. I am in grave danger of becoming an intellectual cabbage (laughter). It's no joke; I know it's a real danger. I get home very late and I don't have time to watch television anymore; not that I ever did much. I don't listen to the radio anymore. I don't go to the cinema and I don't read. It all adds up to an abnormal situation.

Y.B.P.: Do you read the papers?

I look through them. I read the weeklies very quickly. But things cannot go on like that.

Y.B.P.: Being an archbishop doesn't sound much fun!

Well, it's a question of duty. It's not a job I would have chosen, and I don't do it for fun, but because God asks it of me. That's the only thing that makes that sort of life possible in peace of mind and heart.

Y.B.P.: So really it's better to be a parish priest.

Much better!

Y.B.P.: Because one is in direct contact?

That's it. You can preach, say Mass, have discussions with people who have problems with their faith; one can help people in their lives and proclaim the love of God for humankind.

Y.B.P.: Don't you have an official position too?

Not directly. What are you getting at?

Y.B.P.: Aren't you in touch with the government?

Yes, I think I have to do that. The mission I have received requires that I speak out at the right times on issues of conscience and morality. These are human as well as Christian concerns. I don't start off by making a statement to the press. Often a public statement of that sort means that things are past mending (laughter). If one wants to make an impression on a political figure, it's much better to speak to him personally. So I think it's my duty to get to know the leading personalities in the social, political, and economic world so that we can understand each other and size each other up. I hope that the people I have to deal with can see me primarily as a man of God, so that they can appreciate that when I speak, I do so as a believer who is trying to witness to justice, peace, and truth. I need to convince them that I am not defending the interests of a pressure group by means of the political power game. So I think it is my duty to have contacts with the French president, with members of the government, with the opposition, and with members of public bodies.

Y.B.P.: Are Vatican politics discussed at the archbishop's house?

More or less. I mean by that that we are concerned about the welfare of the Church. But we are not directly involved in what the Vatican will say or do about South America, for instance. But we can give our opinion on the matter.

D.J.: How close are your links with the Vatican? Do you send in frequent reports?

Not really, but I am rather new to the game. Some links are part of the institution; so every five years, every bishop pays a visit to the pope.

D.J.: Every five years?

Yes, every five years. The bishops of each country have to go to Rome and give a report of the situation in their country. But John Paul II has started another sort of link. He goes to the various countries himself, and this means that the leaders of the population come together. On particular problems there are special study groups; the national conference of churches delegates somebody. Rome has an age-old tradition where the management of the Church's affairs are concerned. One of the problems after Vatican II was to renew these traditions so that the various national churches could take part in them. One of the major concerns of the present pope is to prevent the Vatican administration from becoming top heavy. He wants to follow the indications of Vatican II so that bishops from all over the world can take part in the government of the universal church and bring their own contribution to it.

Let me give you an example. Canon law is very important. It has been reformed several times through the centuries. The last text dates from 1917; at the moment, it is being recast. For the last ten years, a commission has been working on this, made up of international experts, bishops, and cardinals. Before promulgating it, the pope asked all the bishops of the world to come and criticize the text and to submit it to a final revision.

Y.B.P.: I expect you know that in Israel we have some political parties that are religious parties.

I do.

Y.B.P.: At least three of them, if not more.

Yes.

D.J.: What do you think of this combination of politics and religion?

That question is a trap. I don't want to make a pronouncement on the internal politics of the State of Israel.

Y.B.P.: Would you say that a Christian religious party would always be a right-wing party?

No, it could just as well be a left-wing party. It is quite possible to have a party with Christian ideals that is progressive. But what you are really asking is whether it would be right to transform a democratic state into a theocracy.

Y.B.P.: Our question is about Israel.

It's different with Israel; there the question is more serious because of the religious meaning of kingship in Israel, a meaning that has been inherited from the Bible.

Y.B.P.: We have political parties that we consider to be

extremely right-wing, and they want to impose their rules on the state. Have you followed the affair of the excavations in Jerusalem?
I have.
Y.B.P.: Our "church," if you will excuse the description of the rabbinate, has been in open conflict with the government over it.
How can I answer without sitting in judgment?
Y.B.P.: So what is your considered view on the question?
That you mustn't try to use me to settle your quarrels (laughter).
Y.B.P.: Could you imagine a Christian leader forbidding excavations at a spot where there might have been burials two thousand years ago?
Certainly not.
Y.B.P.: He wouldn't see these archaeological digs as a lack of respect for the dead?
Certainly not.
Y.B.P.: Our religious parties said the opposite. When we attacked them in the newspapers, they said: "But all other religious communities, including the Christians, are the same. None of them allow excavations where there might be bones."
Actually, it's the opposite with us. Pius XII and his successors are the ones who wanted the excavations at the Vatican that are on a burial place. There would only be sacrilege and profanation of the dead if there were an intention of insulting them or if there were lack of respect toward one's beliefs or toward what one cherishes. That was not the case, I imagine. I know that the excavations in Israel caused fierce reactions on the part of Muslims as well as Orthodox Jews. But the excavations yielded fascinating results from the point of view of Jewish and Christian history.
D.J.: When did you last go to Jerusalem?
In 1977.
D.J.: When you go, what sort of people do you meet?
As many people as possible, all sorts of people.
Y.B.P.: Not only church people?
No. I went in different circumstances. For ten or fifteen years, I went nearly every year with groups of students.
Y.B.P.: Were these educational visits?

They were pilgrimages. We went to "discover" the holy places. We also planned meetings with Muslims, Palestinian Christians, and Israelis. We used to have regular meetings at the University of Jerusalem. We always used to visit one kibbutz. We did all the things one does on a two- or three-week visit when one wants to show youngsters a different world from their own. These yearly visits gave me many possibilities for establishing contacts, although, as leader of the group, I did not have much time for making visits on my own. But when I could, I tried to meet people in ordinary life and casually.

D.J.: Did you meet Israeli statesmen?

Hardly, but I met Ben Gurion on his kibbutz.

D.J.: Was that at Sde-Boker?

Yes, but I could hardly claim to have known him.

Y.B.P.: Did you like Israel?

Oh, yes (laughter). What do you mean exactly by "like"?

Y.B.P.: Well, the Israeli solution for Jerusalem?

I would say that the least one can hope for is that the holy places be accessible to all and be taken out of belonging to one nation, in one way or another. This would mean an international guarantee for their accessibility to people from the different creeds involved, Muslims, Jews, and Christians.

Y.B.P.: Are you in touch with the Jewish community in France? Have you met Chief Rabbi Sirat?

Yes, I have met him and also Alain Goldmann, the chief rabbi of Paris; also Chief Rabbi Chouchena. But don't forget I am only beginning my time as archbishop of Paris.

Y.B.P.: Is there mutual suspicion between you and the head of the Jewish community?

I know that some of the things I said were hotly contested by Chief Rabbi Sirat, in certain articles that you obviously know about. But when we met afterward, he was extremely friendly. He had understood what I had said to journalists in a different way from what I had intended; I was not speaking in legal terms. I was using everyday language and expressing my personal feelings and sense of belonging. So I think things have been clarified; I hope so, anyway. As for the Jewish community, I have not really had the chance of meeting it yet. You see, I am not Sephardic; I do have Sephardic friends, but I know the Jews of Europe better than those of North Africa.

Y.B.P.: Is the French Jewish community more Sephardic than Ashkenazi today?[11]

Yes, surely you know that.

Y.B.P.: No, I am not all that clear about it.

Really? Well, in recent years there has been a certain shift in the trends of French Judaism.

Y.B.P.: I am not so clear about things because every time the French Jewish community is mentioned, the name of the Rothschilds comes up, Alain and Guy. And people talk a lot about the Jewish revival, about political conflicts.

You are alluding to Hajdenberg?

Y.B.P.: That's it.

I see. Anyway, I don't know him. Let us say that I have not yet had contacts with the community as such.

D.J.: Could we have just a few more minutes with you? Who would you say are the greatest figures of the Old Testament and what is their message?

I'll take another ten hours to answer that one (laughter).

D.J.: Just quote three names.

Only three? That's not enough. I could say Abraham and Isaac, or Moses and Aaron, or David, or even the greatest sinner among the kings of Israel, or the prophets, or many others. How can I choose? Your question is too journalistic; it is as if you asked me in French literature what my favorite book is.

D.J.: You would say Victor Hugo, alas!

Certainly not (laughter). Really, all the parts of Jewish history convey something of God's revelation and love, his truth, and his message. So it would be very hard for me to choose.

D.J.: I have another question. You lived through the time of the Holocaust and you suffered from it. How do you see the Holocaust fitting into the pattern of history? What is it that made such a thing happen? How can a believer like yourself make sense of it?

In this present world, humanity is struggling with the worst. It is struggling with the negation of itself. In this world, the absolute for which humanity is made and which is its state as divine, has a negation that is its hellish condition that can neither be understood nor endured. In this case of the Shoah[12] (I prefer to say the Shoah rather than the Holocaust, because Holocaust means something else; it is a free offering given to give glory to God), there was the will to exterminate. What was even more unbearable was that not only were human beings massacred and exterminated, as is still happening all over the world today for all sorts of reasons, but they were exterminated for no other reason than that they were Jews. The Nazis had other enemies and opponents, and they did not suffer the same fate for the same internal reasons. The only reason was that they were Jews. It is therefore a crime that goes beyond anything that one can imagine; it is a denial of the other. At the beginning you asked me, "What is a Jew?" I said, "A man who brings the news of God's choice to his neighbor." And here he is being rejected and killed for no other reason. It is the uttermost limit of homicidal hatred. It is only when we see hatred like that that we can see, in its unbearable starkness, the destiny of the Jews and the destiny of humankind. That harsh light gives a glimpse of the dark depths of humanity itself. The only possible response is silence. One cannot talk of such a thing. Nor should one want to, because it is unbearable. The only thing that I can think about it, in my deepest self, is that from what is completely evil, God can nevertheless bring something completely good. I don't know how he will do it, but I believe that all those who are victims of this horror were most certainly well loved by God.

Y.B.P.: One needs faith to talk like that.

I know, I speak as best I can. But there is a further consideration. I think that somehow they belong to the sufferings of the Messiah. How, only God can say, not me. And one day their persecutors will see that it is through them that we are saved. I don't know. I suppose it is better not to say such things. But it is what I think; of course it's not a justification of what happened. Once again Israel is a bearer of revelation; it reveals something about history, and it reveals something about the nature of humanity.

Y.B.P.: But it could happen again.

It could happen again and it is happening again. One trembles at the thought that a disaster like that could happen again. But it is not just an accident; what happened exposes the human condition. We must therefore remain always on the watch. We know now what can exist deep down in human society. So those men who are on the side of goodness and dignity, and who believe, those men must remain always on the watch.

The worst aspect of the whole business is not only that crimes were committed but that men tried to justify themselves for having committed them. So there were two sorts of evil; there were the crimes committed, and of course one already knew about human cruelty. And there was the evil of trying to justify these crimes, looking for the reasons that motivated such acts and finding a cause for them instead of denouncing them; I think that is a greater evil, and it is widespread in our own day. Only the other day someone was trying to explain the assassination of President Sadat by looking for the reasons that motivated the murderers. No one looks for the motivation behind the courage of innocent victims. It is always violence that people are trying to justify. This points to a sort of blackout of the human mind, a kind of veil over people's judgment. The Shoah did not occur in the Dark Ages, in the time of the Huns, and in a remote corner of the world; it took place in Europe, after the great eighteenth century, the century of Enlightenment.

Y.B.P.: I read in a newspaper something that you had said and that struck me as particularly fine. Could you say it again for us and explain it? You said, "My nomination as bishop meant for me that all of a sudden it was as though the crucifix were wearing the yellow star."

I can say it again but I can hardly add anything.

Y.B.P.: By that remark you were paying homage to the Jews who were persecuted and who had to wear the yellow star.

Yes, in spite of themselves and without knowing it, they

became the image of innocence in this world. Without knowing it; no one chooses to be a hero. I know that all those who died over there were not heroes; but since they were persecuted unjustly, they bore the figure of innocence and right. Some people want to deny what happened, the concentration camps, and so on. By doing that, they not only reveal their bad conscience but also their secret desire to deny innocence and to avert attention from it. That is the way things happen in this world. First of all, the flouting of innocence is accepted, and then one denies that there is such a thing. But taking on oneself the image of the innocent victim, that is at the center of the faith of Israel. That is the figure of the suffering servant in Isaiah.

D.J.: Do you, as one of the prelates of the Catholic Church, feel a moral obligation toward the Jewish people?

Of course. But I have always felt like that, and so would anyone, I think. The fact that I have a different office does not make any difference to that feeling or to that duty. I would add that every time there has been persecution of the Jews, there has also been rejection of Christianity. Those Christians who persecuted the Jews, whether they were politicians or churchmen, sinned grievously against God and against the Jews. Their actions amounted to a denial of their attachment to Christianity. It was not a national or ethnic quarrel; it concerns the essentials of the faith, as is shown by the fact that their attitude was often disguised under religious reasons.

Y.B.P.: Do you intend to visit Israel?

I would like to, but I don't know yet.

Y.B.P.: Do you know if the pope is going to Israel?

I don't. He has said that he would like to go, but I don't know exactly when that will be.

Y.B.P.: You don't know?

Didn't he say he was coming?

Y.B.P.: Yes he did.

Well, if he said it he will do it.

D.J.: What sort of man is the pope? He seems very nice, and he is very popular in Israel. Can you tell us how you see him?

Well, first of all, he is an extremely cultured man. To understand a man like that, you have to know something about his past.

Firstly, he is a Pole; everyone knows that, but it implies a particular culture and a historical context that are different from those of western countries. I am sure that everyone in Israel knows about contemporary Polish history, how Poland had to recreate its national identity, Polish nationalism between the wars, and so on. I am sure you understand that better than the French, because you also had to live through the problems of recreating a national identity. So, from that point of view, the pope is in a good position for understanding you.

Secondly, the pope has had twenty years of wartime experience. He was in the Resistance; he was deeply affected by the most dramatic episodes of contemporary European history, much more than the English or the Americans could imagine, or Italians or Spaniards, more than Frenchmen even. His country has been much more deeply affected by the war, by the German occupation, by deportation, and then by the movements of population after the annexation of part of their territory. Lastly, the communist ideology has affected his country.

Thirdly, the pope is a man whose philosophical upbringing has come from German philosophy; phenomenology has been one of the sources of his philosophical thought. These are already three extremely unusual things for a pope to be. So he has a very personal view of contemporary history. He is not an Oriental; he is a man from eastern Europe. But he is a much traveled man; he has visited the Polish Diaspora, which is scattered all over the world, more or less. He has a world vision rather than a Roman one. He is in Rome now, but Rome is no longer the center of the world. The world has its center wherever humanity is. The pope gives symbolic expression to this truth by moving about everywhere.

Fourthly and lastly, he is a mystic; I don't mean in the sense of people who have visions.

Y.B.P.: You mean a deeply spiritual man?

That's it; a man who is completely in the hands of God, so that he is extraordinarily free. He couldn't care less about what people think about him. He never plays to the gallery. He is a free man; someone like that can face any situation; he can also welcome anyone. He is a mystic; he is not afraid.

Y.B.P.: So how can someone like that become pope?

It shows that miracles still happen (laughter). I don't believe in providential personalities, but I do believe that God's providence provides the right man. In that sense people become providential. That being said, it's still true that times and periods change. John Paul II is a different sort of pope. Previously people from western Europe didn't know that beyond the Oder is still Europe. They just ignored that part of Europe that is made up of the Slavic nations. I wasn't surprised that it was the people from the Third World, from Africa and South America, who related readily to a pope from a country that has such a different image. He really is a sign of modern times.

Y.B.P.: Were you already a bishop when you met him?

Yes. I met him several times. Never have I met anyone with whom I have felt more at ease. He doesn't necessarily agree with you, but he is a man who can be completely attentive and who has an extraordinarily well-stocked mind. He understands what you are trying to say because he is so well disposed toward you. But you couldn't pull a fast one on him. He listens in silence, but his supreme skill is saying what he thinks.

Y.B.P.: One more question, rather a fanciful one. Christmas is near and it nearly always occurs at the time of Hanukkah.[13]

Yes.

Y.B.P.: What do the candles signify at Christmas? Is there any connection between the two festivals?

There could be.

Y.B.P.: Could one find a symbolic link between Christmas and Hanukkah that could express the connection between Judaism and Christianity that you have been talking about?

I don't really know. I think the similarities are due to a coincidence, but there could be more to it. It's different with Passover and Easter; they are the same festival.[14]

Y.B.P.: Jesus himself celebrated the Passover, didn't he?

Yes, and Christians celebrate the Passover of Jesus.

Y.B.P.: The feast of Hanukkah came much later.

There are different views about how Christmas came to be observed at the winter solstice. It looks as though originally the heavenly conception of Jesus was celebrated on the same date as his death and resurrection, that is, at the time of Pesach, 14 Nisan, the spring equinox. That would put his birth at the winter solstice. The date was also chosen to replace pagan festivals because all pagan European peoples celebrated the winter solstice. So the feast of the Nativity of Christ was used by the church to sweep away the idolatry of the Romans and the others, and to christianize these winter festivals. There is no historical evidence about the date of the birth of Jesus. I wonder whether my colleagues, the rabbis from Pharisaism, didn't do the same thing about finding a date for Hanukkah (laughter). Someone should study the historical origins of these two festivals. Hanukkah stands for the reversal of history, the overturning of false gods. Christmas may have had that meaning to begin with, thanks to the belief of the Jews and Pharisees that the meaning of history could be reversed. But I really don't know; there is something obscure about the whole thing.

Y.B.P.: Do you have any family in Israel?

Yes, I discovered it after becoming archbishop of Paris. I did not know that I had cousins over there.

Y.B.P.: Did they get in touch with you when they learned that you had become archbishop?

That's exactly it. I received lots of telegrams and letters from cousins whose existence I did not know about. Ours was a very large family. They all said they were first or second cousins. I have one first cousin who survived the extermination and who knows more about the family than I do. He is researching it.

Y.B.P.: Did they send you photographs?

Yes, although not all of them were actually relatives. The name Lustiger is quite common. There were only two or three who were really my cousins. But Armand really is my first cousin, and I was really surprised to learn of his existence.

Y.B.P.: One more question. Do You think that the church could have done more to save Jews during the war?

There is quite a lot of research being done on that. After the event, the judgment that can be made is always different from the one made at the time. Don't forget the attitude of the leaders of the Allies on the question during the war! Both Saul Friedländer and Léon Papeleux have been doing research on the subject; that research must go on. There was a whole Christian network that was created in order to save Jews. I think that the Church saved more Jews than any other social or charitable institution. Of course, that was her duty. Some people think that it took a long time to come around to a condemnation of anti-Semitism. But Pius XI had already condemned it before the war.

Y.B.P.: Do you know what the attitude of the present pope is toward Israel and the Jews?

I am quite sure that historically he is the pope who has had the best opportunity of understanding the situation of the Jews. He has true sympathy because he saw the Jewish situation through the experience of eastern Europe; that is completely different from experiencing it in western Europe. An Italian can only have a very imperfect notion of what the Jewish condition is like. The pope knows about it directly and in a special way because Poland was the focus of Jewry in central Europe; the pope understands the prejudices against Jews and anti-Semitism in its most irrational and anti-Christian form because it flourished especially in Poland and Lithuania. In order to understand the origins of Jewish nationals and Jewish national feeling before the creation of the State of Israel, one has to remember that it was born in Poland and central Europe. On the other hand, the pope has a very high regard for Judaism, and he respects it spiritually.

Y.B.P.: One final question. How do you explain the way in which the State of Israel had such an appeal for Christian public opinion when it was set up?

When it began, the State of Israel was a utopia. Its creation was to be the realization of equity and justice. I well remember what people were saying in Israel in 1950: "Here the police are honest. Here no one cheats...."

D.J.: Things have changed since (laughter).

There was a kind of primal innocence. In Israel then, there were no thieves; there were prisons but no criminals. Israel was intended as an exemplary creation because it inherited the patrimony of the Jews. But later on, the same gap developed as the one we see between so-called Christian nations and their politics.

Y.B.P.: But don't you find that when you read something about Israel in the papers, something about its behavior as a state toward the Palestinians, for example, don't you find that it is always judged very severely?

I do; it's as if the condemnation were doubled.

Y.B.P.: So that means that people expect more from Israel than from other countries?

Yes, that's because people have an idealistic and unreal view of Israel. They still have the view that its founders had, a view that derives from the biblical requirement for absolute justice and truth.

Y.B.P.: But isn't it unfortunate for us if people expect too much from Israel?

Yes, I agree, because Israel, like other countries, cannot help making mistakes sometimes.

Y.B.P.: And committing sins too (laughter).

Yes, sins too. But one must not forget that the prophets of Israel called humankind to repentance.

2
From Despair to Hope

An address to the first Pan-American Conference on Christian-Jewish Relations, São Paulo, Brazil, November 3, 1985. Translated by Jean Duchesne.

Ever since I accepted your invitation, my heart has been filled with both fear and joy. I have accepted it as the will of the God who leads our lives. This is why I want to receive from him the joy that may dispel the fear that arises from my heart. Above all, I want to thank him for the kindness and affection he grants me through all of you, my brothers and friends. I am more touched than I can express, and this is what gives me the strength to speak out.

I. THE SHOAH

The Second Vatican Council's *Nostra Aetate* was published twenty years ago. Last April 19th, representatives of Jewish organizations and of the Catholic Church met at St. Thomas Aquinas University in Rome to commemorate this event. Their intention was to think about the past and meditate together about the future.

1.

Yet, what can be done or said about the past? We would no longer be ourselves if we failed to remember. But how can we live as long as the horror of the Shoah remains "lurking at the door"

(Gen 4:7)? We cannot talk about it, and today we can no longer agree to keep silent. We cannot tolerate hearing historians mentioning it as merely one episode of a war, or teachers trivializing the event, thus making it possible for it to happen again. We cannot tolerate seeing men who, because of their cultural or religious vocation, should bear witness to moral requirements—which is what is needed if divided humankind is to retrieve its soul—so often avoiding any discussion of this monstrous event. This silence is a form of escapism, and our silent pain cannot condone it.

At that meeting, Pope John Paul II insisted on commemorating the criminal plan whose purpose was to annihilate the Jewish people, and that did, in fact, result in the extermination of millions of us before and during World War II.

"I fully realize," the Pope said, "how timely this commemoration is now. For it is precisely the lack of faith in God—and, as a result, the lack of love and respect for our fellow men and women—that can bring about such disasters. Let us pray together so that this may never happen again, so that we may bear witness to the only one God, and so that his will, as it is expressed in the Ten Commandments, may help make men become ever more aware of the abyss into which humankind can sink when we fail to recognize the others as brothers and sisters, because they are the sons and daughters of the same heavenly Father."

The Shoah happened forty years ago, but for our generation it is still today. We are survivors, and we know it. But we do not know why. What we have undergone nearly dragged us into the madness of our tormentors, as nothing made sense any more.

When we turn to the younger generation, to whom it is our duty to speak about what has happened, we have to confront anew the depths of the deadly abyss into which we have been plunged. The young do not really seem to understand what we still do not manage to express today. And we lose heart when facing this unbearable enigma, this obsession, which is so heavy that we hesitate to burden the young with it.

However, how could we not tremble when we realize how unaware they are of the perils of today's history? In spite of their courage—or in spite of their rebellion—might not the younger generation fall into the same abyss? Should we speak out or remain silent? The Shoah overwhelms us. Israel, the prophetic people, unveils in its own flesh the unbearable mystery of iniquity that the world into which we have been cast is capable of.

2.

And yet, the biblical Word answers the questions that haunt us. For it tells us prophetically about the people whom God has chosen for himself. These words cannot but return to our memory.

How many times during those years have we been tempted to ask the question: "Is it nothing to you, all you who pass by? Look and see if there is any sorrow like my sorrow" (Lam 1:12). And beforehand, we knew the answer: "Zion stretches out her hands, but there is no one to comfort her" (Lam 1:17).

This we had known for thousands of years. We had already experienced the incomprehensible shock: How—*êkha*?[1]—can women "eat their offspring, the children they have borne?" (Lam 2:20).

We knew, because Nebuchadnezzar threw Shadrach, Meschach, and Abednego into the blazing furnace (Dan 3:19–20).

We knew, because the joyful laughter of Purim still shakes with Mordecai's sobs.

We knew, because the divine Word had warned us: "Just as there were many who were astonished at him—so marred was his appearance, beyond human semblance" (Isa 52:14). "He was oppressed, and he was afflicted, yet he did not open his mouth; like a lamb that is led to the slaughter, and like a sheep that before its shearers is silent, so he did not open his mouth" (Isa 53:7).

Among our generation and among our fathers' generation, many would have liked to shake away the yoke of such memories. Was it impossible to stop being a nation apart and to become at last a people like all others (1 Sam 8:20)? But what did we want to forget? Was it what we had become? Or was it the one who had made us? The question remains, and the answer can only be a prayer:

"Restore us to yourself, O Lord, that we may be restored; renew our days as of old" (Lam 5:21).

3.

"How—*êkha*?" God's incomprehensible will creates a shock. But also: "why?" Why this curse in the hearts of the nations? Why did they commit such an impiety?

How could we have imagined that the night would become so dark that we would have to whisper: "My God, my God, why have you forsaken me?" (Ps 22:2; Matt 27:46). Yet when we question him, it is he who questions us.

But we also have the right to question our tormentors and their accomplices, whether they were willing or not. We have this right because it is our duty. Not as victims turned accusers. For who can probe men's hearts? And can a victim become a judge?

Still, we can and must speak as a people of priests (Exod 19:6). We are responsible for those who curse us as well as for those who bless us. With the promise, "I will bless those who bless you, and the one who curses you I will curse; and in you all the families of the earth shall be blessed" (Gen 12:3), our duty and our right is to extract the blessing, not the curse, from the hearts of the nations. We do this so that we may receive the blessing that is as irreversible as the election promised to our father Abraham and to his faith.

The Shoah has hit the Jewish people both in its flesh—a third of its members perished—and in its spiritual strength—how many hassidim, how many pious sons and daughters of Israel have perished while confessing "*Shema Israel*"! But the Shoah has also hit the souls of Christians.

Allow me to develop this point. How could former Christians deny their faith to such an extent that they committed such a transgression? How could those who had received—or whose parents had received—on their foreheads the indelible mark of the hope in the Messiah and been granted its first fruits thanks to their faith, how could they curse the divine name and break the covenant to which they had by grace been given access? Their denial was threefold. One: they disobeyed the First Commandment, "You shall not murder" (Exod 20:13). Two: they strove to destroy the very root that sustained them (Rom 11:18), the people whom God had appointed before Pharaoh: "Israel is my first-born son" (Exod 4:22). Three: they thus disowned the son of David in whom they had believed and through whom they had become children of God when they had heard the divine voice saying, "This is my Son, the Beloved; with him I am well pleased; listen to him!" (Matt 17:5).

Perhaps our own impotence to speak out can help us understand why the King of the nations remains silent (Isa 52:15). This silence is due to sin. Only God can change human hearts and open them up to repentance. It would be blindly presumptuous of us to fancy that human beings can, all by themselves, settle such conflicts and deal with their aftermath. For this is nothing other than the strange fight against God or for God. This fratricidal fight is a deadly affair, which no one can control or put an end to once human responsibility is engaged. The issue is no other than sin. And we know the remedy: "Who can forgive sins but God alone?" (Mark 2:7). When the fullness of mercy blots out the misdeeds (Ps 51:1), when the Almighty substitutes hearts of flesh for the hearts of stone (Ezek 36:26), a sign is given to us that the Divine Spirit is being sent and that new life is being granted to the earth (Ps 104:30). Then the prophetic word begins to be fulfilled: "Stand up and raise your heads, because your redemption is drawing near" (Luke 21:28).

The *Nostra Aetate* Declaration was written in this light, as an act that we must call "sacerdotal." It was like a spiritual offering for the sins of the nations, inviting them all to repentance. This commitment, John Paul II said, is binding us all. This contrition and this commitment are the source of our hope.

II. *NOSTRA AETATE*

As this year is devoted to reassessing the Second Vatican Council's *Nostra Aetate*, I would like to make a few points in this regard.

1.

In Caracas last January 27, when answering to the words of welcome addressed to him by Rabbi Isaac Cohen in the name of the Jewish community of Venezuela, Pope John Paul II spoke very strongly: "I wish," he said, "to confirm with utmost determination that what the church taught during the council in the *Nostra Aetate* Declaration always remains for us, for the Catholic Church, for all bishops and for the pope, a teaching that must be obeyed, a teaching that it is necessary to accept not only as something appropriate, but much more as an expression of faith itself, as inspired by the Holy Spirit, as a word of the Divine Wisdom" (*Osservatore Romano*, January 29, 1985). And a few days later, on February 15, when receiving a delegation of the American Jewish Committee led by its president, Howard L. Friedman, the Holy Father deliberately repeated the very same words he had uttered in Caracas as they sprung from his heart, without having them written down beforehand. And he added: "Let me repeat what I said. These words express the commitment of the Holy See and of the whole Catholic Church to what is taught in *Nostra Aetate*, and they underline the importance of this document. Twenty years later, the wording itself remains timeless. It is clearer than ever that its theological foundation is solid, and that it provides a sound basis for fruitful dialogue between Jews and Christians."

2.

These words I make mine today. I first want to recall the genuine uniqueness of *Nostra Aetate*. Never, since Paul of Tarsus and the Council of Jerusalem, had the Church acknowledged so plainly the vocation of the Jewish people from which she is issued and which exists face to her.

The Church's teaching concerning Judaism goes back to the Council of Jerusalem, which sought to establish rules so as to give the Gentiles access to God's salvific plan by referring to a halakhic[2] principle. Later on, there was the decision taken against the Gnostics and Marcion to recognize all of the Hebrew Bible as God-inspired

Scripture, as the guarantee of both the unicity of God and the Christian identity. There also was the threefold principle established in 598 AD by Pope Gregory the Great and later used as a norm of church law: "No forced conversions of Jews, no attacks on their synagogues or their celebrations, mutual cooperation in civilian life" (see H. Grisar, *San Gregorio Magno*, Desclée, 1904, p. 343). Yet these rules did not prevent Jewish identity from being erased from Christian consciousness during the course of the Middle Ages. In addition to this forgetfulness, there were various discriminatory measures that became the source of grave acts of injustice.

Of course, this long period leaves the impression of an icy silence, especially since, historically speaking, hostile attitudes have unfortunately outnumbered the few expressions of friendship and fraternity. But this silence gives us, for the present time and for the times to come, the space and freedom to speak in truth.

3.

This is what, in my opinion, the Second Vatican Council did when it invited us to the hermeneutic revision that was required for a change in our attitudes. *Nostra Aetate* rejected the notion that the Jewish people "might be cursed or rejected by God, as if this resulted from the Holy Scriptures." The council's declaration has urged us to give up a much too widespread way of reading the Scriptures, one that appropriates it as if the people of Israel had not been historically the first to be elected by God. Vatican II did not say all that could have been said, but there is no dodging the actual significance of the *aggiornamento* that the council asked for. This is what the Holy Father called "the commitment of the Holy See and of the whole Catholic Church."

What is expected from Christians and Jews today is that we both learn to understand each other to the same degree that we each understand ourselves, despite all the changes that twenty centuries have wrought. We must draw upon a mutual understanding of each other that is rooted in our common heritage, that continues despite past struggles, despite the great ordeal of the Shoah, and in the face of the present world's idolatry.

Let us rediscover our common roots. The Bible contains the eternal Word, and promises that remain to be fulfilled. As the American bishops underlined it in 1975, chapters 9 to 11 of St. Paul's Epistle to the Romans have been neglected for too long—and, in my opinion, they were for too long unduly separated from chapters 1 to 8. This is why we have forgotten that Paul insisted on the sturdiness of the promises made to Israel. We must pray ceaselessly that we may better grasp the design of the divine wisdom: the established and always new covenant between God, the master of creation and history, and his people, the universal mission of this people, and its messianic accomplishment among the nations.

In their *Orientations* for Catholic-Jewish dialogue published in 1983, the Brazilian bishops thus recalled that it was God himself who had wanted the Jewish people to exist. It is he again who wants us to turn together to the hope he opens up to us.

III. THE FUTURE

Christians and Jews are linked forever by a common responsibility in human history. And the name of this responsibility is hope.

1.

The first reason for hope I can see lies in the fact that we both bring to the world the same fundamental message—a message of liberation. This message is no utopia, but the truth. It does not concern the future but is already valid today. What it announces is not simply a revolution, but redemption, the salvation of humankind. This message is the word of God, buried like a seed in the earth in order to bear fruit. This seed has been sown on the American continent, and it is no accident that we should have gathered here today, to meditate together on the hope that is arising like a harvest all over Latin America.

Whom can the poor trust nowadays? Where can those in need—or the victims of the multiple oppressions brought about by modern, technological, urban industrialization—find any support? There will be no answer to this question until we have done all we can to fight injustice, to promote the initiatives and the solidarity that are required against all kinds of excesses. God has entered a covenant with his people. He has seen their plight (Exod 2:24–25). He has remembered them and freed them from their slavery. This liberation, which the Jewish people experienced once and for all, is both its past and its future. Through faith in Jesus Christ, the same liberation is offered today to all people of good will. It must develop its power to change and sanctify, for the benefit of the poor who expect the recognition of their beauty, their dignity, and their liberty as children of God.

2.

The second reason for hope is that we are drawing ever closer to each other in our fight for human rights and in a growing awareness of all that these rights really mean. Of course, every human being yearns for justice and freedom. But as soon as human beings are confronted with concrete situations, it quickly becomes obvious that there is no more unanimity. Some governments even invoke human rights to legitimate their own abuses. Even more shockingly, some movements refer to the same rights to justify terrorism, so that international relationships are being undermined by this threat, which comes from the reckless, excessive use of armament. All of this only manages to paralyze moral conscience.

Experience has taught us that human rights are fragile, that they are often applied in a contradictory or even arbitrary way. So a lot remains to be done. We believe that the only rock on which human rights can be grounded is our rock: the God who has created human beings in his image and resemblance.

We are thus invited to share the task of bearing witness to the significance of human rights. For Jews as well as for Christians, any infringement on human rights is a transgression of God's law. Fighting for the respect of the rights of every human creature is a religious duty; it is obeying God's law. As Pope John Paul II said to the IJCIC representatives who had come to Rome in 1979,

"Every time Jews recite *Shema Israel* and every time Christians recall the great first and second commandments, we draw closer to each other by God's grace."

3.

The third reason for hope is that Jews today can live in a country of their own, according to their ideals and their wishes, under principles and laws that are theirs.

Christians are not unconnected to the causes that have led so many Jews to seek shelter in this place that all of us call the Holy Land.

Going back to the land that God promised in his covenant does raise a number of formidable, contradictory questions for Jewish consciousness in the spiritual, ethical, and political spheres.

What still-hidden divine plan is being accomplished through this? What as-of-yet unheard call will complete the promised gathering? What answer will spring from the hearts of the sons and daughters who, in their parents' dreams, no longer bear the stigma of the past? There is no one who can say (Ps 74:9).

The pressures of the present times, with all their conflicts, seem to indefinitely postpone answering these stubborn questions. With the singularity of its history the Jewish people, again becoming a nation on its own land, must obey the precepts that impose themselves on every human conscience. All the rights that one claims for oneself must also be acknowledged for others. Those who have heard that all human beings have been created by the one Lord of the universe know that they have to assert that all men are brothers. Was it not God who inscribed in every man's conscience the love of justice as the foundation of all rights? But if peace is to reign, the violence of history must be overcome and all wounds must be healed.

I can see a sign—and I believe that it was deliberate—in the fact that John Paul II chose Good Friday last year to evoke Jerusalem's yearning for peace and to affirm that Christian consciousness acknowledges the State of Israel's right to existence, with all that this right implies. The Holy Father said: "For the

Jewish people, who live in the State of Israel and who safeguard in this land such precious testimonies of their history and their faith, we must demand the security and the just tranquility that are the rights of any nation, the conditions that are necessary for life and progress in any society."

Jerusalem bears the word "peace" in its name. It remains eternally the symbol of the peace that the whole world hopes for, and it remains the place where this hope is at stake.

3
Judaism and Christianity

An interview from *Choosing God, Chosen by God: Conversations with Jean-Marie Cardinal Lustiger*, by Jean-Louis Missika, Dominique Wolton (1987). Translated by Rebecca Howell Balinski, Ignatius Press, 1991.

THE PAGAN TEMPTATION OF CHRISTIANITY

DOMINIQUE WOLTON: *Can we go back to your discovery of Christianity?*

It was as though I knew about it already. Not its customs, rites, practices, but its content. I seemed to have understood it beforehand. I was even surprised when other people did not understand what I understood. I continue to be, by the way. Those affirmations touching on the mystery of God, the meaning of the revelation through Christ, God's call to humanity—to his people—are all evident to me. They are a part of the logic of faith, and I am stupefied to discover that there are believers, steeped in Christianity since childhood, who do not understand this.

WOLTON: *Do you have an example?*

Oh, many! The Eucharist, the Mass. Even though I had not had a Jewish education, I knew enough to recognize the ritual of the Passover in the Eucharist. It is the sacrifice of the lamb, of the suffering Messiah; it is deliverance and salvation, the grace of God. When I discover Christians who have lost this reference and no longer understand the Eucharist, I say to myself: they are pagans. They do not know what they are saying or doing or how much they are in contradiction with what they are supposed to believe.

Another example: my memory of the first Holy Week in which I took part in 1941 is still fresh. I went with a group of classmates to an Oratorian seminary in Montsoult. For three afternoons, we joined the community in singing the office of Tenebrae, a service made up of psalms and biblical readings. Chanting the psalms, listening to the Lamentations of Jeremiah, I felt it was obvious that Catholics were sharing the inheritance that God had initially destined for Israel, the elder son, the firstborn.

WOLTON: *You saw a definite continuity between the two?*

I saw more than continuity. At last, I was able to grasp the solution to what had been insoluble problems. I mean, the key to the enigma was given to me, in a new mystery: the mystery of Christ, the crucified Messiah.

The continuity is marked in the texts of the revelation and in Christianity's use of the Bible. In the chapel at Montsoult, there were stained glass windows depicting the relationship between the two Testaments. Also, at the cathedral in Chartres, I was able to greet holy King David. At Germigny-des-Prés, a Carolingian church, I joined the angels who, in the mosaic in the apse, are worshipping the Ark of the Covenant.

I was not in alien country. I was one of the older sons. I did nothing more than begin to enjoy the heritage that had been promised to me. Only much later was I able to express more precisely what I had immediately understood intuitively: the problem of God's relationship to pagans and Jews is at the heart of all Scripture, of both the Old and New Testaments.

WOLTON: *To pagans and Jews, admittedly. But to Jews and Christians?*

But they have the same history. The problem raised by Saint Paul and practically all of the New Testament writers concerned "Christians," "Messianics," who, both Jews and pagans, had entered into the new covenant of the Spirit. One of the proofs that the Messiah has come is that pagans also have access to the covenant because the Spirit has been given to them. Through faith, they too can unite themselves to the king of Israel. "In Christ" (that is, in the Messiah), according to Saint Paul's expression, all fulfill the precepts of the law and share in the new covenant where they obey God, thanks to the gift of the Holy Spirit. In other words, the promises regarding the universality of God's reign are on the way to being carried out.

WOLTON: *You mean fulfilled.*

"Fulfilled"? The word is too ambiguous and has stirred up too many arguments. It is acceptable only if it conveys a sense of plenitude, of obtaining the full measure of what has been promised. But this realization evidently implies an internal mutation and choices. The question of Israel's historic destiny and its election, the question of the destiny of the Jewish people was at one time an obsession for me, and it still is in some ways. It is completely different from the question about the Basques' or Bretons' relationship to the French nation. It is a question that involves the salvation of humanity. Some people will diagnose my obsession as Jewish paranoia. I wish to emphasize that I am purely and simply a believer.

WOLTON: *Do you really believe that most Christians share your point of view?*

Pagans, even when they become Christians, are constantly tempted to refuse the particularity of history and divine election. They are tempted to make Jesus the projection of the ideal man that each culture and civilization creates within itself. That is the most instinctive way of bringing God down to man's scale—in other words, of falling into idolatry by worshipping oneself. Each pagan civilization that becomes Christian is likely to be enticed into making Jesus its Apollo and projecting its own image of man, an image that it finds pleasing.

Christ himself, the figure of Christ in its reality, can assume every face of humanity, but that can happen only because he is first of all the individual who was born in Bethlehem of Judea. A phrase from Saint Matthew can enlighten us: the Magi who arrive are pagans and they ask, "Where is the King of the Jews?" He has to be searched for, and in the end, after scrutinizing the Scriptures, they find him "in Bethlehem of Judea," and not somewhere else. And it is Jesus they find, not "an" infant, but "this" infant. Thus, the contingency of the absolute is the very form of revelation.

Fundamentally, the mystery of God's becoming human flesh remains an almost insurmountable contradiction. A rational mind can dismiss it as a myth, something that will not stand up to logic. After all, what does God-man mean? The mystery is of the same nature when God speaks with Moses "as one speaks to a friend" (Exod 33:11), and it deepens when the Word of God makes itself human word and inscription on the two tablets of the law. It is very difficult for our minds to conceive that the transcendent communicates himself. Is it possible that he who is beyond all representation, who cannot be imagined, can become accessible? Certainly man can conceive that there is another side to the frontier that his thought has established. He can say to himself that although he has determined that frontier, every limit has a beyond that is greater than all thought, too great to be imagined. But transcendence, as it has historically revealed itself in person to the Jewish people, is the Almighty whose initiative literally stuns the human mind: it places it vis-à-vis God. God is not simply the "no-man's-land" beyond the limit that man himself has discovered and will have to cross sooner or later.

God's revelation manifests the presence of the one who presents himself in person as absolute subject, in the face of whom man himself materializes as subject. It is the revelation of the one who is both Creator and Redeemer. The inconceivable declares himself, he says who he is, and makes himself accessible to man. That act drastically changes the human condition and in a sense even annihilates it: "Then I will take away my hand, and you shall see my back; but my face shall not be seen" (Exod 33:23). God also says to Moses, "You cannot see my face; for no one shall see me and live" (Exod 33:20). And, simultaneously, this presence gives substance to man by saying to him who man is, thus allowing him to live accordingly.

The fact that God presents himself and speaks to Moses "as a friend" is already the mystery of the incarnation of God's Word who makes himself our flesh, makes himself known to us, and gives of himself. And the fact that the Messiah is the eternal Son of

God made flesh is also a metonymy: he is Israel, not by substitution, but by inclusion. He is the one in whom the filial condition of the holy nation is realized. Jesus observed and fulfilled the commandments given by God to Moses for his people, Israel. He faultlessly fulfilled what had been required of the Jew for living in holiness—a holiness required for the salvation of all nations, for the redemption of the sons of Adam, for bringing together and uniting all that divine generosity has spread and lavished on the world. Through him comes deliverance from sin and access to life.

WOLTON: *Is what you have been saying obvious to Christians?*

It is difficult for Christians to recognize Jesus' Jewish roots. Some of them would reason that Christ chose a country, a civilization, a culture, a language, and that as Christians, we must love what Christ chose. But there is something absurd about such reasoning if it implies that Christ, in his condition and human will, was able, unlike other men, to choose the time and place of his birth. The eternal Word of God became flesh in Mary, daughter of Israel, because God his Father had previously chosen Mary's people and had confided his name and his Word to them. Christ was sent in the fullness of time. He was expected by God's people and was to be recognized by them. In plain language, Jesus could not simply pick a place and date for his birth. It was not by preference or chance that he was born in Bethlehem rather than Lutetia or Rome. If he was going to be recognized as the "King of the Jews" and the envoy of the unique God, he could be born only in Bethlehem. That this title is often ignored or refused, not by the church, but by a certain number of Christians or Christian generations, is a sign of forgetfulness, of a grave deficiency in thinking; indeed, it is a sign of sin.

WOLTON: *Yes, but this forgetfulness has lasted a very long time and has had considerable effects….*

Forgetfulness is always blended with memory to make tip the moving forces of human history. Each Christian generation is characterized as much by its blindnesses as by its intuitions. That explains why entire peoples can drift along over long periods in situations that have no exit. For example, there were those barbarians who were both Christians and Arians,[1] meaning that they did not believe in the Son's divinity. Other examples can be found in Christianity's internal divisions, the separation of the churches of the East and the West, or what happened in the sixteenth century at the time of the Protestant Reformation. Thus, today there exist various and sundry ways of being Christian. Over time, these differences have been transformed into cultural elements and are transmitted by education. That this can be so remains an enigma. Either these blindnesses, these omissions are normal divergences in mankind's history, or else they are departures from faith, departures from fidelity to the faith. I happen to believe that they are the latter.

CONTINUITY AND NEWNESS

WOLTON: *Do you think of Christianity as being a fulfillment of Judaism?*

There you go with that word again. "Fulfillment" has many meanings. Of course, human history is not finished. According to the Bible, we are in a time of the covenant and a time of passage. For Christians, the coming of Christ and his paschal mystery renew the divine covenant and give man full access to God. In his Messiah, God fulfilled the promises made to Israel. And the Scripture again uses the expression "the fullness of time" for announcing the return of Christ and his glorious manifestation. Fulfillment connotes all that.

WOLTON: *But in religious history, the Word is often used by Christians to define the relationship between the two religions.*

We cannot speak in terms of chronological stages that would determine ruptures or continuity. For the Christian faith, the coming of the Messiah is a divine intervention. It was previously announced, promised, and prepared. The novelty of this visit by God does not annul the preceding divine interventions: it attests to them and reveals their universal, divine significance. God did not go back on his promise when he revealed in his own Son what had been hidden in his chosen people and what, in the resurrection of his Christ, became the eternal nouveauté promised to Israel and hoped for by all the sons of Adam. It is in this way that the new covenant realizes the divine Testament whose promises it makes "old" as well as fulfilled. There is a traditional adage: "The New Testament is hidden in the Old; the Old comes to light in the New." The question remains throughout time: Are these divine revelations to be recognized and welcomed, or are they to be refused?

WOLTON: *Fine. I am going to word my question differently. Why is it that most Christians find it so difficult to accept what you see as the natural link between Judaism and Christianity?*

Throughout the Christian tradition, there are witnesses to and precedents for a belief that you seem tempted to attribute to me alone, or to the church after Vatican II, or else to regard as something entirely recent. The link between Judaism and Christianity has never been broken, and the understanding of the relationship between the two Testaments has never disappeared.

I suggest that you look at Father de Lubac's work on the meaning of Scripture.[2] In excavating the treasures left to us from the patristic age, he shows us ways of understanding Scripture and its present relevance. He brings together a wealth of citations from early and medieval authors, and, in particular, he demonstrates that the opposition *carnal-spiritual* is not the equivalent of the distinction between the Old and New Testaments. There can be a "carnal" understanding of the New Testament, just as there is a "spiritual" understanding of the Old. The Messiah, Christ, frees us from the carnal understanding and initiates us into a spiritual one because in his person he is the new and eternal truth of the covenant and of all its structure and development. The theological tradition that teaches this has solid support, but its opposite can also be found, because theories on the "deicidal people" and their rejection of Christ have been formulated and expounded.

JEAN-LOUIS MISSIKA: *It is the theories on the deicidal people that have dominated for quite a long time.*

Yes, but it is essential to verify the context in which they were nurtured. I do not have the historical competence to do it. However, it does seem clear that the state of theology, of the evolution of Christian thought, can be assessed by its positions on the subject of

Israel. I believe, for example, that Luther's anti-Semitism is not innocent and has something to do with his nominalism.

WOLTON: *Are you saying that, at any given moment in history, support for the theory of a discontinuity between the Old and New Testaments reflects a weakness of theology?*

Yes. It is a sign of perversions and divergences. Theology is not a neutral science. It is the means by which men try to articulate the contents and implications of the revelation with the aid of the Church's Magisterium. At the same time, it is a source of progress for human thought since, in confronting the mystery, it fertilizes the fields of philosophy and anthropology. But the theologian's understanding of the revelation is commensurate with his capacity for thought. By that very fact, his own fidelity is subjected to a terrible ordeal.

There is always discontinuity where sin and death reign. But the continuity of sacred history attests that God's faithfulness is ever greater. To sum it up, the Christian tradition witnesses to the continuity of God's plan and his fidelity to the election of Israel. But, in spite of significant examples, this witness has often been overshadowed. Saint Augustine's works are sometimes tinged with an anti-Semitism that is considered aggressive today because we read his texts with an awareness of Luther's rereading of them. Simultaneously, in the *City of God*, Augustine shows a remarkable understanding of the continuity of the history of salvation. What he says may seem new to you. He declares that all that has been said and given to the Jews is a part of the history of salvation and remains offered to them irrevocably. What is offered to the Jews, he says, is a grace that spills over to Christians of pagan origin, allowing them to enter into the covenant and to come to know God through the deeds of the Messiah, his Son, and through the gift of the Holy Spirit. Everything that Augustine says there has belonged to Christian thought from its origins.

MISSIKA: *That may be so, but it was the Church Fathers who theorized Christian anti-Semitism.*

To some extent, I agree. But you cannot read Saint John Chrysostom in the light of *Mein Kampf*. No! That would be grossly anachronistic, and it will not hold up historically. Let us go into more detail. In the tradition of the church fathers, there were certain ones, like Saint John Chrysostom, who spread intolerably hostile notions about Jews. But in the same tradition, there exist texts that have such a strong theological and spiritual continuity with the Old Testament that today it is impossible to know whether they are Jewish or Christian. And do not forget that the early church adopted the psalms as its prayers.

There is anti-Judaism in that tradition. But the traditional polemic with the synagogue was a dispute between inheritors. It was not a refusal of the heritage—which makes it completely different from modern anti-Semitism. It is just not the same thing! Christians reproached Jews for an infidelity to the faith and tradition of Israel that they recognized as being of divine origin. But the Nazis loathed the Jews, their faith, and their traditions with an equal intensity.

On the religious plane, the overshadowing of the relationship between the Testaments and the contempt for Jews are always signs of a grave deficiency among Christians. In the second century, a heresy led by Marcion wanted to suppress all references to the Old Testament, to purge from the Scriptures all mention of it. No one would dare to call himself a Marcionite today, but Marcionism remains latent and sometimes explicit in Africa and Asia. Cardinal Ratzinger has recently reminded us of this. He was referring to people who, under the pretext of affirming their cultural roots, say, "What do we have to do with the Jews? Our Old Testament is our traditional culture." But, in that case, Jesus risks becoming a black Apollo or an Asiatic Hercules.

WOLTON: *But in the Church's history, it is rather the tendency that has insisted on the rupture and difference between time Old and New Testaments that has dominated.*

I beg your pardon! History and sociology may support your opinion, but it is not true from the point of view of faith and theology. I am not forgetting the persecution of Jewish communities in medieval Christianity. But the points of view must be distinguished.

The Church Fathers remind us incessantly that Moses was speaking to Israel in the name of God. If they criticized Jews, it was for being unfaithful to their vocation and their own Scriptures. The Church Fathers knew the Bible by heart. There has never been a Christian Bible without the Old Testament.

I am not saying that Christian thought has always been perfectly unequivocal on the matter or that it has not also undergone temptation. Every man is tempted. Where did Hegel come from? Where has all that thought—often rationalist, often gnostic and, thus, anti-Jewish, come from, if not from the temptations of the West? But these thoughts are found just as often among Jewish thinkers. Spinoza is a rather well-known Jew, and there is a celebrated Hegelian called Marx. In fact, the history of religious thought and the history of humanity merge, and men are forever tempted and tried in their freedom. History is not static. It is freedom and the adventure of the human mind that test our faith.

WOLTON: *Precisely. Why is it that there has never been a general council on this fundamental question of the relationship between the two Testaments?*

Because the relationship has never been contested. Many important beliefs have never been defined by a council because they were never questioned. They are truths so confidently possessed that an authenticated definition has been unnecessary

WOLTON: *Looking back on my religious education, I recall that the Old Testament was never forgotten, but its position was inferior to the New.*

Were you taught that the liturgy refers to "Saint Abraham"?

WOLTON: *No, "Saint Abraham" was never mentioned!*

Of course, you were not taught to say "Saint" Abraham. But in the thirteenth century, he was invoked. I asked the question because I knew what your answer would be. In fact, since the seventeenth century there has been an overshadowing of a certain number of similar elements that were previously a part of the church's everyday teaching. Take iconography. The representation of the synagogue in church architecture is not limited to the blindfolded figure on the cathedral in Strasbourg. And even there, the synagogue is shown as the sister of the church. There are also figures representing the holy patriarchs, the tree of Jesse, and all the honored prophets who are venerated along with the evangelists as spokesmen for God. What I am telling you reflects the concrete position of the church. The people who built the cathedrals were not on the fringes of society! The images we see there were not conceived by a few eccentric or clandestine church members. This iconography represented "official" thought. It is significant, too, that Saint Thomas raised the question as to whether circumcision could be considered a sacrament. And he also reflected on how the doctrine of the sacraments could be applied to the faith of the Old Testament. I am reminding you of all this so that you understand that it would have been completely inexplicable if the ecumenical council of Vatican II had suddenly published a text that changed church doctrine and thus contradicted all that Christianity had taught up to that time! Such an occurrence is impossible, by definition.

But what, from the nineteenth century I think, was called anti-Semitism remains to be explained.

CHRISTIAN ANTI-JUDAISM AND ATHEISTIC ANTI-SEMITISM

MISSIKA: *Yes, it began to be called anti-Semitism in the nineteenth century. For the preceding period, it is more accurate to speak of anti-Judaism. But the change of words does not preclude their association. Besides, the word anti-Semitism makes no sense.*

None at all. It is a great pity that Pius XI chose to say, "We are spiritual Semites." Although he meant well, he conceded too much to anti-Semites by acknowledging their category. But he was using the language of the times in his protest against Nazism.

It seems to me that we have to go back to the eighteenth century to understand the problem. It was then that, in western Europe, the emancipation of Jews and the rise of modern anti-Semitism began simultaneously. What was the prevalent attitude of the philosophers and preachers toward Jews? In both philosophy and religion, there was a theology of the Enlightenment that was extremely summary, and there were also the first signs of an anti-Semitism of the Voltairean type. Why was Voltaire such an anti-Semite?

WOLTON: *What would you answer?*

My answer is that Voltaire, although a product of Christian civilization, is not Christian. And I believe that Hitler's anti-Semitism had its roots in the anti-Semitism of the Enlightenment and not in a Christian anti-Semitism. I do not know if historians have pushed their analyses that far.

WOLTON: *You really believe that there cannot be Christian anti-Semitism….*

I believe that profoundly. There can be antagonisms, there are heartbreaking conflicts. The Church can disagree with Judaism as far as the Messiah's person and the salvation of nations are concerned, but there is no anti-Semitism of the Voltairean sort—that is, an intolerance toward the Jewish existence in its substance, toward the Jew's power of revelation.

MISSIKA: *Meaning?*

A refusal of the Jews' divine election, a hate for their religious singularity, which is considered irrational and hence unacceptable. In looking at this question, the anti-Semitism of Voltaire and Diderot must not be discounted. It was their current of thought that created feelings of shame in German Jews during the eighteenth and nineteenth centuries.

WOLTON: *Then Christians are absolved?*

I did not say that. But one fact must not hide another. It is essential to observe the spiritual histories of societies and to understand how they are modified by the values pursued.

Until the eighteenth century, the spiritual history of the West merges with the history of Christianity. Throughout this history, Christianity's relationship to Judaism is a test of its faithfulness to its source. Thus, Christianity's annals record both the faithfulness and unfaithfulness of Christian nations to this source. It is a record of sins and of God's mercy toward peoples to whom he gave the grace to receive the revelation. Even ideal societies—I mean by that particular communities founded on an ideal of holiness: religious orders, for example—have histories that are made up of sin and reform, of periods of decadence and rebirth.

My thesis is that, yes, spiritual history is marked by anti-Semitism. By its very nature, Christianity cannot be anti-Judaic, but the anti-Semitism of Christian nations has to be explained. By the way, I count Voltaire—as well as Hegel and Marx—among Christian thinkers. They were all inheritors of Christian culture. Christianity was a part of their backgrounds whether they liked it or not. They are lost children, rebellious children, but they spoke the language of the Christian West. And Nazism was born among a people who had been baptized. But Nazism was a refusal of Christianity, a pagan resurgence. Official Soviet anti-Semitism is also of this nature. They are both fruits of the same rationalism... and too many Christians have succumbed to it.

WOLTON: *You are saying that anti-Semitism has deeper roots in atheism than in Christianity?*

They cannot be separated like that. The explanation has to be all-encompassing. The West has been marked by the Jewish as well as the Christian tradition. Then why has it treated Jews the way it has? This maltreatment is a sign of its crisis. And in citing certain influential Western authors who are rarely included in the history of anti-Semitism, I am making the point that modern, rational, atheistic thought is anti-Semitic. More so than Christian thought. Modern anti-Semitism is bound to be radical because it is an antitheism. The Church, on the contrary, in being strictly faithful to her message, can resist and condemn the anti-Semitic practices of Christian peoples, the social injustices, the persecutions and exclusions of minorities that are born of jealousy, self-righteousness, envy, or ambition.

WOLTON: *And why can atheism not do this?*

Because atheism cannot accept that the Jew is the figure of the Absolute, present in a contingent revelation, in the specificity of history. Whereas Christianity speaks of the humiliated Messiah, Maurras,[3] who is no longer Christian, speaks of "Jewish venom" that the Church spread in spite of the Roman Empire. That is also what Hitler said, and the Stalinists: One must be wary of Jews. Just as one must be wary of Christians. Atheism cannot tolerate the particular presence of the Absolute in history. The only absolute it can admit is in men's hands. For the atheist, the Jew will never be reliable, unless he, in turn, declares himself to be an atheist. Otherwise, he is a potential traitor.

MISSIKA: *But why should atheistic thought be more anti-Semitic than anti-Christian?*

Because it can always attempt to harness Christianity by proposing that it become a national religion. It can try to secularize Christianity and hence reduce its influence. But the Jews are on the margins of society, they are "foreigners." As Jews, they remain "unsecularizable," unassimilable. Admittedly, with the Enlightenment a certain secularization of Jews began. But almost three hundred years later, Jewish "foreignness" continues to set them apart. It may be possible for Christians to think temporarily that they are sheltered from such threats, but they should make no mistake about it, as Maritain said, "when Jews are persecuted, Christianity is menaced in its flesh." As proof, it suffices to evoke the nihilist invectives, so common in modern literature, against Christ as a figure of cowardliness and resentment, the figure for the religion of the weak.

MISSIKA: *I wish to make an objection. A little while ago, you made a comparison between early Christian anti-Semitism and pagan or atheistic anti-Semitism dating from the Enlightenment. It should be noted that the former has had a much longer time to do its harm. All the anti-Semitic themes, all that has been said about Jews for the past twenty centuries, was articulated between the first and fifth centuries, especially by the Church Fathers. The carnal Jew, the worshipper of the golden calf, the thief, the fiendish Jew, the trafficker—not to mention the Jews who spilled the blood of Christ. If Voltaire is anti-Semitic, it is because his writings echo a theme that was perfected in the polemic of the early Christians against the synagogue.*

No, a pagan anti-Semitism, predating Christianity, did exist.

MISSIKA: *I disagree completely with what you say. Jules Isaac's*[4] *work on the genesis of anti-Semitism clearly shows that there was no real anti-Semitism before Christ.*

Well, then, we disagree. Pagan anti-Semitism has to be explained. Why were the Romans so fierce in pursuing the Jews?

MISSIKA: *Because the Jews resisted.*

Yes, they were the only ones to resist ancient paganism when it clothed itself in political authority.

MISSIKA: *They were simply a people who fought back.*

It was more than that. Take another look at such authors as Théodore Reinach and Marcel Simon.[5]

MISSIKA: *Extracting what Roman authors said about Jews does not make sense unless the citations are compared with what was said about other peoples, the Gauls or the Greeks, for example. If all non-Romans are scorned, it is impossible to speak of a specific anti-Judaism in antiquity.*

But your examples do not date from the same period. The ancient pagan anti-Semitism penetrated the Church after Constantine. Some of its themes were purely and simply taken over by the Church at that time. Such themes are completely absent from the New Testament. There are traces of the ongoing religious conflict in the Scriptures and in the first writings of the Fathers, but the nature of the conflict was different. As far as I can see, the institutional opposition to Jews began with Constantine. It was then that things began to take on another face. It is important to situate the precise date—and it is not to exonerate Christianity that I say this—when the political conflict between the Synagogue and the Church began. It happened coincidentally with the union of the empire and the Church, and the disappearance of the Jewish Church in Jerusalem.

MISSIKA: *There was also the problem of competition between the religions.*

Yes. Throughout the first century, Christianity was a Jewish affair. The religious competition between Jews and Christians was very keen. Then came the conflict with Rome and the problem of Israel's permanence as a people. Although Jewish proselytism existed throughout the Roman Empire, the physical existence of Jews as a people was being threatened. During the first Christian century and again at the beginning of the second, those who were called "the Jews" were Jews of the synagogue and their proselytes, while the others, who were called Christians, were Jews who believed in Christ and were united in the churches with the pagans who had been converted to the Gospel. We must not project onto the religious argument of this period, which was indeed sometimes harsh, the one that came into existence later, at the beginning of the fifth century.

MISSIKA: *You have cited Saint John Chrysostom. What he says is interesting because he invalidates the often-advanced thesis that there existed a popular anti-Semitism that the Church Fathers—or, in any case, the priests of the epoch—were forced to go along with. Saint John's polemic against the synagogue was intended to dissuade Christians from going there, to dissuade them from consulting rabbis for answers to moral questions. He was struggling against a fusion, against the building of any bridges between the synagogue and the church.*

Yes, but there is also Saint Jerome who consulted the rabbis because he wanted to learn Hebrew in order to translate the Bible into Latin.

MISSIKA: *Nevertheless, was it not at that time that all the main themes of anti-Semitism took shape?*

That is partly true. What I challenge is a completely uniform vision of history that would maintain that for twenty centuries, Christian anti-Judaism and atheistic anti-Semitism have been one and the same. The Jewish minority was always physically menaced, and it is a fact that an ideology of conflict was elaborated. But it is false to say that this ideology has remained unchanged from 30 AD to the end of the twentieth century.

MISSIKA: *But it did crystallize during the first millennium.*

There were exceptions. Some believers said and did the contrary. How do you explain Córdoba? How do you explain the first Poland?

MISSIKA: *I admit that there were exceptions. But even so, the system generating the decline in Jewish-Christian relations was set up during the first thousand years. What happened afterward was simply the continuation of that policy of contempt and degradation.*

I repeat, I am not convinced of that. The periods must be delineated more clearly. I would almost be ready to concede that what you are saying applies to the period that extends from the eighteenth to the twentieth century. Within these years, there appeared an ideological anti Semitism that has engendered great turbulence and unspeakable crimes. I am not saying that there were no disgraceful injustices in previous periods—the accusations of ritual murder, the *rouelle*,[6] the segregation, the Marranos.[7] But, during the first thousand years, all of Christian Europe claimed the heritage of Israel; it was even proud to the point of jealousy. Christian generations reproached the Jews for not being faithful to their fathers and their prophets, but they never doubted the sacred history of Israel. Projecting the modern ideological radicalization of atheistic and political anti-Semitism onto a religious past when Christians and Jews venerated the same heritage, would reflect a serious misunderstanding of Western history. The old anti-Jewish polemics are certainly not sufficient for explaining the concentration camps.

MISSIKA: *And you do not believe that there is a link between the two?*

There is more to it than that. The Nazis wanted to exterminate homosexuals, the physically and mentally handicapped, and the Gypsies as well. They also wanted to annihilate the Poles in concentration camps. Their contempt for man was directed at all sorts of men. But the Jews, as figures of election, caused jealousy and catalyzed on themselves the Nazis' negation of man and God.

WOLTON: *Would you go so far as to say that, in the ideas that led up to the concentration camps, atheistic thought had more responsibility than Christian thought?*

Atheistic thought is a temptation born of Christian thought. Only someone who has been confronted with the question of God can be an atheist. Only a Jew or a Christian can become an atheist. A Buddhist cannot become an atheist like us. Moreover, the source of this atheism must be specified. Does it come from Christians in general? From theologians? From clerical political parties? And what are the responsibilities we are talking about? Do you mean to say that churchmen should have been more lucid? In their particularity, the Jewish people carry the heart of the revelation. And in a certain way, they also bear the image of the Messiah, of Christ. The way nations or generations treat Jews is an indication—this is my personal conviction—of how they treat Christ, of what they really think of God. What they do to Jews confirms what they do to Christ. What is said against Jews condemns those who say it. All this goes well beyond the economic, social, or political aspects of the matter. If Jews are singled out for persecution, it is not only because Christians have elaborated specific arguments against them. It is because Jews carry within themselves that which is most sacred and, hence, least tolerable to others: the sign of divine election. That is why anti-Semitism cannot be completely assimilated with racism and xenophobia. Anti-Semitism is one of the most serious spiritual questions in all of history.

JUDAISM TODAY

WOLTON: *How do you view Judaism and its relations with Christianity?*

I have no authorization to express Judaism's opinion of Christianity.

MISSIKA: *I propose a solution. Suppose we take a dispute from the Middle Ages between the Church and the Synagogue. Very often these disputes between priests and rabbis focused on the following question: "Has the Messiah come?" One of the rabbis' arguments was: "Is it possible to affirm the Messiah's presence in a world where Jews are suffering so much?" How would you answer that argument today?*

The rabbis' question is pertinent. I would like to say a few words about both the question and the response.

The Messiah is a suffering Messiah. For Christians, his coming is an enigma, something incomprehensible, paradoxical, because the Messiah in whom we believe is humiliated and crucified. His work of redemption is still hidden, and history is not finished. As for the rabbis, when they speak of messianic hope, they are evoking the completion of history. The Hassidic movement, with its great diversity, foresaw something else; it more or less identified the Messiah with Israel. To the question of how one can say that the Messiah has come if Israel is still suffering, Hassidim's response—at the most extreme point of Israel's suffering in the eighteenth century, just as the Enlightenment is bursting forth at the dawn of modern times, which are going to bring the most violent wave of anti-Semitism ever and the Jews' most cruel ordeal since the destruction of the temple—is completely astonishing: the messianic subject, as they describe it, is Israel identified with the suffering Messiah. At least, that is the way I interpret their point of view. The Christians' Messiah is a humiliated Messiah; he is presently hidden, his glory is concealed, in his disciples and his body. His glory is with God, because the end of history has not yet come. The messianic hope is given in this continuing history, and Israel still has its role to play in it. The Messiah's hidden role in which his disciples, the "Messianics"—that is, Christians—believe and the role or the mission of Israel have something mysterious in common. That is why I said that the rabbis' response was partly right: the Messiah will come again in glory. But why did he have to suffer before entering into his glory? It is a formidable question that the Apostles, the first disciples, themselves came up against. And it was then that their spiritual "healing" took place because their act of faith, a gift from the Spirit, restored their sight, healed what the Gospel calls a blindness or a hardening of the heart. Christ's disciples eventually understand that it was necessary that the Messiah suffer before entering into his glory—and even now, in the members of his body, his suffering continues. History had to go on, and it had to be a history, not of errancy and despair, but of compassion and redemption.

MISSIKA: *Then Israel (and hence Judaism) has its* raison d'être *as long as the Messiah has not come in glory?*

Yes, Israel has its *raison d'être* until the coming of the heavenly kingdom.

MISSIKA: *In spite of Christianity?*

The "Christian" category does not erase the categories of Jew and pagan; the church does not deny the differences, she relativizes them by referring them to Christ.

MISSIKA: *But what about the Jew who is completely disinterested in Jesus? Is he in error or in truth?*

In error or truth? It is not man but God who can answer that question.

WOLTON: *Let me word it differently. What meaning does the Christian give to Judaism's presence today?*

Well, Saint Paul articulates the answer for us. The Jews, the Jewish people, exist because God has chosen them. They have no other reason for existing, not even national sentiment. Otherwise, we would be able to give a socio-historical explanation by saying that the Jewish people's survival is of the same order as that of the Basques or Hungarians. Not for one second do I accept this kind of explanation. The existence of the chosen people concerns God's plan for humanity: if Israel exists, it is because God has chosen this people for the purpose of saving all mankind. But election is not so much a privilege as a mission.

I mention in passing that Nazism perverted the notion of a chosen people in order to create a diabolical messianism of their own. It was not subjected to God, but on the contrary looked to the coming of the Superman and thus to the annihilation of the rest of humanity. Nazism identified "election" with domination and unconscionable privilege.

To come back to your question, it is God who has favored Israel. God brought it into existence for the salvation of all humanity, for the coming of the reign, and, according to the promise, it is in Israel that the Messiah, suffering, has already appeared. Until the Messiah's coming in glory, the Jew remains, and he remains a Jew, whether he is Christian or not.

WOLTON: *But the Jew who is Christian accepts the Messiah, while the one who is not refuses him.*

It cannot be said that Israel did not recognize the Messiah. The original Church, after all, was a Jewish Church.

MISSIKA: *But that was never in doubt.*

But it was! It is a historical truth that was obscured for a long time! The research of the past fifty years, in various domains, has brought this back to light. The Jewish Church was first leveled by the Byzantines and then by Islam; hence, it was twice destroyed. The Chaldean Christians, whose liturgical language is Aramaic, say that they are the direct descendants of the Jewish communities that bordered the Euphrates. Some people claim that the present Melkite Christians represent the Semite Church in the East. They were twice assimilated, but they survived. They adopted the Byzantine rite while the other Churches kept the Syriac liturgy—whether Chaldean, Syrian-Occidental, or Antiochene (more or less influenced by the surrounding culture with its Byzantine and Latin elements). Moreover, they also adopted Arabic, whereas the other groups kept their own languages in the liturgy. These Christians are perhaps the remnants of that first church.

Why did the totality of the Jews not recognize Jesus as the Messiah? It is a tough and troubling question. Saint Paul reminds us of God's patience, men's sin, and their redemption. I ask a corresponding question: "Why did the totality of the pagans not recognize the Messiah that Israel was awaiting?" Because neither have all pagans entered into the covenant—far from it.

MISSIKA: *But if you reason in quantitative terms, Christ's message has nevertheless had more success with pagans than with Jews.*

That does not make much sense. Beyond a certain period, no comparison is possible. In the third century, the Jewish Church ceased to be identified as such; it no longer had a legitimate place. There are both a sin and a tragedy in that fact. The term that Saint Paul uses to characterize the relationship between Jews and pagans is "mutual jealousy": the pagans deny the existence of Israel, and Israel is afraid of losing its specific identity and special relationship to God. The fear of merging with others and disappearing is a legitimate fear, and Israel's survival by God's fidelity remains a testimony inscribed in the history of God's irrevocable gifts and calls. But the fear of acknowledging that pagans also can receive the grace of the covenant is something else, because that promise had already been made by the prophets—Amos, Hosea, Isaiah, and Jeremiah. The promise that pagans will come from Egypt, Assyria, and elsewhere to worship the living God is found in all of them.

MISSIKA: *And the crucifixion?*

I refer to Saint Paul. People are always saying that it was the Jews and not the pagans who crucified the Messiah. But that is simply not true. According to Saint Paul, he was crucified by all men. At the time the evangelists were writing, the argument with the synagogue was intense; nevertheless, the accounts of Christ's passion in the Gospels and the Acts of the Apostles place the responsibility for the Messiah's death on all men, Jews and pagans.

Saint John gives a prodigious presentation of the dialogue with Pilate, a dialogue that most of the time we tend to forget. We think of Pilate as a colonial governor who was dealing with the natives while understanding nothing of their affairs. That is simply untrue. The Roman law represented the highest ambition of rationality and justice, and yet Pilate is going to commit, from the legal point of view, an absolute denial of justice. It is he who carries the juridical responsibility, and it was Roman soldiers who crucified Jesus. The pagans showed themselves to be sinners in a situation where they were pretending to observe the law, just as the Jews did not recognize the one whom it was their mission to recognize. Human history is that way; it is filled with injustices and infidelities.

But the measure of the grace of forgiveness and mercy that the Messiah brings is infinite. The revelation of every man's sin that takes place through him is not made for condemnation but for liberation, as long as this light available to man—namely, the recognition of his sin is accepted. If he refuses it, he closes himself into his blindness. But the Messiah's light is a gift of mercy. It is constantly being offered. Through the human condition of his own Son, of Jesus, the unique one, God "has redeemed all sin." Israel was already a much-beloved son and remains so.

WOLTON: *On that point, I would like to know how you feel about the thesis (defended in particular by René Girard) that says that Jesus divested the sacrificial mechanism by consciously offering himself but that afterward the Church, by a sacrificial interpretation of the cross, fell back into mythology by accusing the Jews of having killed Christ and thus restoring the mechanism of the scapegoat.*

From the point of view of Catholic theology, that argument does not hold up. Imagine a child who has never seen a Jew in his life; he does not even know if such people exist anywhere in the world and has heard about them only through the Gospels. What will his reaction be if people say to him, "You see, those wicked Jews killed Jesus"? That argument is based on a crude interpretation, too summary as to facts. Any Christian who reads the Gospel is going to have the same reaction as Pascal. He is going to hear the crucified one say to him, "I shed this drop of blood *for you*." And, like Saint Paul, he will say, "he loved me and gave himself up *for me*," for my sins. The believer recognizes in the crucified the one in whom everyone's refusal to turn to God is represented and also the one who delivers us from our refusal. In other words, whoever pretends that he is innocent of that death, that it is the "others" who killed him, cannot believe in Christ. His attitude is even a proof that he does not believe, because to believe in Christ is to have a "broken heart." It is to conform to the image of the fifty-first Psalm and to Jeremiah: the hardened heart becomes "a broken and contrite heart" through the greatness of God's love, which wants to forgive, so that the heart of stone becomes a heart of flesh.

In Christ's death there echoes another question whose full depth is perceived only by someone nourished and instructed by the Bible: Why do the just suffer? This lamentation is heard already in the book of Job. Israel never ceases to raise the question, obstinately, all the while maintaining, against all obstacles, the idea that if man obeys God, he attains his happiness. That idea is profoundly true, but it is paradoxical and sometimes almost unbearable because the just do suffer. "What have I done, Lord? Surely you know! Then why do you hide yourself? Why do you not speak? Why do you remain silent?" The just one suffers, the Messiah suffers, and we are all responsible for his suffering. Every Christian recognizes himself as culpable for Christ's death. If he does not, then he is not Christian. Saying that "it was not I who did it, it was somebody else," is placing yourself outside of Christianity. That is why anti-Semitism, in its pseudotheological version—"it is the Jews, not us, who killed him"—is blasphemous. It denies the uni-

versality of redemption. It refuses to see in the face of the crucified—the son of Israel unjustly persecuted—God's power, which
reveals everyone's sin so as to be merciful to everyone.

WOLTON: *What would have happened if all Jews had recognized Jesus as the Messiah?*

I cannot envisage something that does not precisely belong to
us—that is, a picture of eschatological times.

WOLTON: *But as far as the history of salvation is concerned, is the fact that Israel still exists the proof that the Parousia*[8]
has not been realized?

Yes, and Israel is a guarantee of the Parousia's coming.

WOLTON: *Then Judaism bears witness to an unfinished
history?*

Yes, but not like some archaeological fragment.

WOLTON: *Would it not have been possible, except for
accomplished eschatology, for all Jews to convert to Christianity?
What would happen if, by a kind of miracle, Judaism recognized the
Messiah?*

Who can speak in the name of all Jews? Your supposition
resembles a little what the Hassidim say: for the Messiah to come,
all Jews in the world must, at a given moment, be perfect saints.

WOLTON: *That gives us a little time!*

Your irony has such a nice smell of skepticism. You understand that my point of view is different. For me, it is a matter of the
work of redemption. Besides, the Hassidim say that Jews must be
either perfect saints or complete sinners. The question remains. It
does not belong to us. Saint Paul says, in his Letter to the Romans
(I am quoting from memory): If the Jews' refusal took place for the
reconciliation of the world, what will their reintegration be like? It
will be like a resurrection of the dead. In other words, the Jews are
not a people called to experience something that would be alien to
them, something unprecedented. They are a structural part of the
history of salvation; if all Israel recognized the Messiah, that would
mean that all other nations would also have recognized him.

Christ is the messianic subject: Christ and his brothers. His
brothers are those who are born in him through baptism. The rite of

acceptance is baptism. Those who enter the new covenant do it not by circumcision but by baptism. John the Baptist's baptism became the baptism in Christ's name. It is given to all, Jews and pagans, and henceforth signifies this: we have all been at fault; we have all broken the covenant. None of us, Jew or pagan, is worthy of the gift made to him. To enter into the new covenant in the Holy Spirit, the one announced by the prophets, we must receive this baptism, the baptism of repentance preached by John the Baptist for the remission of sins. It is the baptism that the Messiah performs in the Spirit. And this rite of acceptance and renewal is also a rabbinical rite. Look at what happened in the state of Israel when the rabbis insisted that the Falashas[9] be formally recognized as Jews.

WOLTON: *The Falashas were opposed to it.*

Rightly or wrongly.

As messianic subject, Christ is composed of all those who belong to him through baptism and by faith. And in a certain way— I repeat, in a certain way—the Jewish people are a part of him: "According to the flesh," as Saint Paul says. "According to the flesh" does not mean solely according to biology or the continuity of carnal generations; it also connotes an always promising and always too short moment in the history of salvation.

Not so long ago, I heard a charming but exceedingly naïve song, a Christmas carol from Normandy. The words went something like this: "Had he been born in Bricquebec, we would have loved him very much. With the Virgin Mary," etc. I find those words amazing!

WOLTON: *Why?*

Well, because they show an incredible lack of comprehension of the Christian mystery! In the first place, he was not born in Bricquebec.

WOLTON: *Do you have something against Bricquebec?…*

No, but I find the hypothesis reflects a profound misunderstanding. It seems to be saying that "we" in Bricquebec would have behaved better than the people in Bethlehem, because we are "good" …and not "bad" like them.

THE DOCTRINE OF THE WITNESSING PEOPLE

MISSIKA: *I would like to come back to a point that seems important: you have developed a variant, or an updating, of a theological point of view going back to Saint Augustine, the doctrine of the witnessing people. Most of the time, however, Jews challenge this doctrine; they do not like it very much and some say that it is anti-Semitic.*

I was not speaking of a "witnessing people" in that sense but rather of a people who are actors in the history of salvation. Judaism is not an archaeological site, not an Indian reservation that is preserved so that one can say: That is the way they used to live.

WOLTON: *But you do acknowledge that this doctrine was widespread in the Church for a long time.*

Yes, but it also had a positive meaning.

MISSIKA: *Even for Saint Augustine? "They have become our book bearers," is a very well known phrase. "They have become our book bearers in the same way that slaves march behind their master carrying his books."*

Yes, but many of Saint Augustine's other remarks convey a better understanding of both the dignity of the people to whom the Bible was entrusted and its mission in bearing witness to the truth.

MISSIKA: *I also have a similar quotation from Pascal: "It is necessary for the proof of Jesus Christ both that the Jewish people survive and that they be miserable because they crucified him." This sentence leads me to conclude that very often the doctrine of the witnessing people is accompanied by the idea that their decline is essential for proving the truth of Christianity. The Jews have to be here, but in a wretched state….*

What you have just said belongs to the arsenal of fantasies that, as far as I am concerned, is completely unworthy of Christianity. Such affirmations, not to speak of such condemnations, "forget about" the universality of sin and redemption. What does remain true is the enigma of Israel's separation. But a setting apart is a holding in reserve. The one who is set apart is hidden in God's hand, in view of his plan. In spite of its infidelities, Israel remains beloved until finally, the time of tears that is man's history having ended, all of Israel, "Khol Israel," discovers the totality of the redemption. All of Israel means both the living and the dead. To understand this forgotten dimension of history, you have to be open to a religious vision that escapes cultural and rational consideration. I do not see what the universality of salvation could mean if it did not include the dead—those whom we call dead—as well as the living. "All men" refers to all who are held, somewhere, in the divine consciousness, in the heart of the one who is the Creator and Redeemer of all. Otherwise, we are nothing more than a swarm of midges swallowed up by evolution and time. If the dead do not count, if they have no right to human dignity, to human existence, religion loses its meaning. The human condition cannot be reduced to the biological condition that is perishable, precarious, and perpetually challenged, a condition in which individual existence is less stable than the existence of the species. Such a vision, basically materialistic, takes no account of the human spirit or the hope that is in man. Every Jew hopes for Israel's conversion, and Israel's conversion means the turning back to God of the whole of Israel.

WOLTON: *Could you clarify that point?*

When Jesus says that the suffering, whether directly imposed or brought about by indifference of any of his brothers, will have been inflicted on him, he is speaking of those who will have become his brothers in baptism, but perhaps also of all those who, in the coming generations, will be sharing "according to the flesh" his messianic mission. There is a connection. Nevertheless, Israel is not, through itself or itself alone, a substitute messianic subject.

MISSIKA: *There is something I still cannot understand. Do you consider Christ's message universal? In that case, are those who ignore it not in error? On the one hand, you say that they are not, that their nay can be legitimate, and on the other, you maintain the universality of the message.*

You are forgetting history or, rather, time's duration. Mankind's history is unfinished. The Church is the sign and sacrament of salvation for all humanity. By the Church I mean the assembly of the Messiah, the body of the Messiah, the spiritual body formed by all the Church's members. At present, the Church of God is at work in human history, like yeast in dough.

You say to me: If you are Christian, you think that Christianity is the truth for everybody. I reply: Yes, of course. You conclude: Then those who are not Christian are in error? Here you are confusing the true and the false. The adhesion to the truth about which the Church speaks is not identical to the recognition of a mathematical principle. Her truth is a revelation, and it redeems sinful human freedoms so that they can participate in divine life. The revelation spreads itself like life. Not every partial revelation or partial truth is mistaken. In the first place, divine truth is God who calls and commands. It is accessible only to the extent that man lets himself be seized by God and receive what God ordains, to the extent that man is delivered from his blindness and sin. Divine truth is the mystery of God's Word speaking first in Israel's history and then becoming flesh in the Messiah and giving of itself through the Messiah's brothers.

While on this subject, I remind you of one of the great scandals for the Christian mind; it tormented believers for centuries: What is the place in the history of salvation of those people who have not been evangelized? This scandal burst forth in the West when it was discovered that it did not cover all of mankind's history. How do you inscribe in the history of salvation those who, in good faith, died without knowing about Christ, without baptism, without hearing the Gospel?

WOLTON: *That is something like the question about children who die without having been baptized.*

Exactly. It is the same question.

WOLTON: *And what is the response?*

In the first place, it is the secret of God and his mercy! We are not to substitute ourselves for God's justice. God alone is judge. Who are we to judge? This kind of debate allows us to understand a great deal. To say that the last days, eschatological times, have begun is not to deny history but to confirm its unwaning gravity. The Messiah's glory remains hidden in God, and man's history goes on. Hence, the births and deaths, the uses of knowledge and speech, the multiplicity of languages—everything that makes up the human, corporeal, historical, ethnic, and national condition remains in God. Nobody can claim to give the divine and authorized vision of these historical developments. Saint Augustine attempted this meditation in the *City of God* at the time of the Roman Empire's collapse. From century to century, thinkers have been fascinated by the question of how to give a spiritual interpretation to universal history. This is just as true of Jewish thinkers as of Christian ones. The coming of the Messiah awesomely deepened the question rather than suppressed it. It confirmed and demonstrated the universality of the biblical message that affirms that we are all made by the same Creator and Father and that, hence, all men are brothers. It is a fantastic affirmation that breaks with so many primitive mythologies according to which "we" are men and "the others" are not. In the unique human history, it is not just those who recognize Christ as the Messiah who work with him for the world's redemption.

MISSIKA: *You consider that Judaism also works toward that redemption although it does not recognize the Messiah?*

The Jewish people were and are still the inheritors and witnesses to God's promises and Abraham's faith. Those promises are irrevocable. Believing in the promises associates them with the plan for salvation.

WOLTON: *But did the new covenant not invalidate the preceding one?*

Neither of the covenants ever expires.

MISSIKA: *Then why would Christianity be useful to Jews? If I follow you, it is necessary only for the pagan nations.*

Is it not important for a Jew to know who the Messiah is and to hear the Word of God? Is it not important for everyone to know what we are still hoping for?

Why and how does anybody recognize the Messiah? That is the mystery of God. An act of faith is a grace from God who offers himself to each person's freedom. Faith is born in men's hearts by the gift of the Spirit.

WOLTON: *We would like to present you with a quotation from Franz Rosenzweig, who wrote* L'Etoile de la rédemption *and* *holds some positions quite close to yours on relations between Judaism and Christianity. On the brink of conversion, Rosenzweig stops; he does not step across the threshold. On the contrary, he affirms his Judaism and, after a dramatic night, he writes, "It is impossible; it is no longer necessary." And a little further on he explains that Christianity is a Judaism…for pagans.*

WOLTON: *Yes, for pagans. What do you think of that observation?*

It is equivocal, because it can be interpreted in at least two different ways. It is true that Christianity is Judaism for the pagans, *in the sense* that, for the Christian, it is in Christ that Judaism receives its plenitude and recompense by making God accessible to pagans. And pagans can believe in Israel's Messiah only if a part of Israel has, by faith, recognized its Messiah, God's Messiah.

But there is *another meaning* that is unacceptable. It amounts to saying that Christianity is a product for exportation, something of reduced value, intended for the nations who have rejected idolatry, so that they can receive a certain justice and have a share in an elementary covenant—a "Noachian" covenant made by the Creator with his creatures of flesh and blood. I do not need to go into the reasons for which this latter interpretation seems to me to be erroneous and dangerous. It suffices to say that the essential is passed over in silence: the Messiah and the Holy Spirit are given to all the sons of Adam.

4
"Let My People Go!"

Address by Jean-Marie Cardinal Lustiger at Yale University, November 2, 1992. Translated by Jean Duchesne.

I have a favor to ask you: at the end of this lecture you don't have to bother to tell me that I have disappointed you. I already know it! And I *do* intend to disappoint you, for I am not going to deal with any of the subjects that I have been told you would like me to tackle.

Of course, "Let My People Go"—the title I have given for this address—does conjure up something. First, the eternal longing of the people of Israel. Next, the lot of African Americans. Or maybe both?

Anyway, I am not going to talk about the diplomatic relationships between the Vatican and the Israeli State, or about the Carmel of Auschwitz, or about the Shoah, or about anti-Semitism in Germany or France. I have already spoken up on these subjects. You must know or guess how I feel about all this.

And I am not going to tell you my own personal story, as the *New York Times Magazine* did a few years ago. If you want something more substantial, just have a look at the book that was recently translated into English under the title: *Choosing God, Chosen by God*.

The most burning and difficult questions in today's politics are raised by the rebirth of nationalism. The recent Roman synod of European bishops has endeavored to cope with this serious problem. People usually don't think of confronting current political issues with the contents of the Bible and the message of the Gospel. And when such confrontations do occur, they generally reveal age-old prejudices and blatant distortions.

This is why I am appealing to your memory. I would like to suggest that current events cannot be fully understood without making reference to the role of Judaism and Christianity in history. As our modern historians say, it is no longer enough to depend on the more recent recollections of the West, based on the French and American revolutions. But older collective remembrances must be evoked, including the relationship between the East and the West.

Let us start with a simple fact, which is at the same time evident and generally neglected: the way most nations see the Jews, or the people of Israel.

"Ah, here we go," you must be thinking. "This is precisely what we had been expecting. You are going to deal with anti-Semitism."

Please do not confuse me with Jean-Paul Sartre!

It happens that I have recently reread his small book called *Reflections on the Jewish Question*. It was published in France in 1954, but Sartre himself says he finished it in October 1944. When it was originally released, thank God, I threw it away after perusing only a few dozen pages. I had only vague recollections of the central thesis. In Sartre's own words, it was this: "A Jew is a man whom the others consider as such. This is the simple truth one must start with." A little further, Sartre wrote: "It is anti-Semitism that makes somebody a Jew."

I forced myself to read all of the 150 short pages of this book. And even now, I remain stunned. Never have I read anything more cynical, more perversely cunning. The whole book deals with anti-Semitism. Or rather, it develops an anti-Semitic vision of the Jewish condition. And the Jews themselves are given no other choice than to struggle for the classless society—where, at long last, thanks to the victory of Marxist dialectics, the Jewish question will eventually disappear, since the Jewish condition is presented as a mere by-product of social contradictions and class conflicts.

In the rest of the book, Sartre proves to be perfectly ignorant of the spiritual matrix that gave birth to the Jewish people and that still moulds all those who claim, or are said, to belong to it. In his narrow-mindedness, Sartre only duplicates the worst prejudices of the French bourgeoisie between the two World Wars. His analyses are savagely to the point. Yet, they offer nothing to the Jews themselves but a reflection of the most devastating images framed by the nineteenth- and twentieth-century French mirrors.

By the way, Sartre was merely echoing Marx's pamphlet issued in the *French-German Annals* (*Deutsche-Französische Jahrbücher*) of 1844. I quote:

> As soon as society has managed to eliminate the empirical essence of Judaism (that is to say trade and its financial support), it becomes impossible for the Jew to exist, because his conscience has no object left.

This man, whom so many people considered a prophet, added that the emancipation of Jews was to be the liberation of society from Judaism, that is to say, from "the 'jealous God' of Israel, whose name is Money." In short, if Judaism was the plague, the socialist revolution was to be the cure.

But enough on this sad subject. Let me go back to my point.

♦

As a matter of fact, there is something correct in Sartre's notion, and this is what I would like to explore. I do not mean to say that it is the other's viewpoint that makes a person a Jew. But since the Second Vatican Council's Declaration *Nostra Aetate* of October 28, 1967, and the instructions for its implementation of December 1974, Christians have been taught how to think about Judaism and the Jews: the latter must be listened to, and understood as they understand themselves. This is certainly good methodology, but the problem might only become more complex, since the descendants of Jacob are endlessly debating what Judaism means today and what definition of a Jew could be given.

The point I want to make is that there exists, in fact, a universal image of the Jew, and that, as a spiritual, cultural, social, and historical reality, Judaism is present practically in the whole world, even if there may be countries where no single Jew has ever lived or is now living any longer.

Why and how is this so?

The reason has its distant origin in ancient Judaism, as early as the second century before the Christian era, when the Bible was translated into Greek—and, we can now say, into excellent Greek. This is what we call the Septuagint, because (according to the legend recorded in the Letter of Aristeas) it was thought to have been the work of seventy Jewish scholars of Alexandria in then-Hellenistic Egypt. Thanks to this translation, a number of learned people—and at that time all of them were interested in spirituality—became acquainted with the ideas contained in the biblical revelation. Many of these ideas were completely new, but they did meet and even surpass some of the questions that had been raised by Greek thinkers—questions that were being discussed at that time in intellectual circles.

Even before the destruction of the Temple of Jerusalem (in the year 70 AD) and Emperor Hadrian's determination to annihilate the people of Israel (between 132 and 135 AD), the followers of Jesus, who saw him as the Messiah and God's anointed or Christ, spread out the treasury of God's Word among the "nations—the "goyim" in Hebrew. Prompted by the same Holy Spirit who had inspired the prophets, the disciples of the Messiah invited the nations to participate in Israel's covenant. You certainly remember the words of the prophets, as they were first addressed to the Hebrews:

> I am coming to gather all nations and tongues; and they shall come and shall see my glory, and I will set a sign among them. From them I will send survivors to the nations, to Tarshish, Put, and Lud—which draw the bow—to Tubal and Javan, to the coastlands far away that have not heard of my fame or seen my glory; and they shall declare my glory among the nations. They shall bring all your kindred from all the nations as an offering to the Lord, on horses, and in chariots, and in litters, and on mules, and on dromedaries, to my holy mountain Jerusalem, says the

Lord, just as the Israelites bring a grain offering in a clean vessel to the house of the Lord. And I will also take some of them as priests and as Levites, says the Lord.

This is from Isaiah 26:18–21. Similarly, we find in Micah 4:2: "And many nations shall come and say: 'Come, let us go up to the mountain of the Lord.'"

Since then, the Torah, the texts of the prophets, and the other writings of the Holy Scripture have been spread all around the world as God's Word. The Bible has reached the most remote peoples, as the vehicle and confirmation of the good news of Jesus Christ that we announce. The Bible is the most widely translated book in the world. It has been translated into 1,685 languages, if my information is up to date.

In spite of the dramatic multiplication of the translations, the Hebrew document (which was later beautifully established in the Massoretic text with its vowel points) remains as the primal text, inspired from on-high. All Christians go back to this Hebrew version as the revealed source and the unchallenged original of all further renditions.

Whether one likes it or not, whether the Jews as well as the pagans—that is, the nations—enjoy it or not, this unparalleled process introduces the singular story of the Jewish people into the universal history of humankind. Not only the events of the Jewish past, but also the spiritual experience of the Jewish people. For the Bible does not simply record the high deeds of a few sovereigns, as the Egyptian or Babylonian chronicles do. It rather demands to be read as God's Word, providing human beings with precepts, calling them to sanctity, and disclosing the depths of wisdom. It also teaches that there are spiritual battles to be fought ceaselessly. Above all, it broadcasts throughout the world the voice of the one and true God, may he be blessed.

The peoples who read the Bible as the expression of the truth thus receive the revelation of the one God of all nations. This is why they cannot but think of Israel's God as the only God of all humans and then their own God. And whether they want it or not, any Jew is then perceived among the nations who read the Bible as belonging to the people through which God reveals himself.

The argument of any pagan for or against God, or for or against his idols, is thus bound to become, sooner or later, an argument for or against the Jews. This concept may not allow us to predict all of the unpredictable turns that history can take, but it has become part and parcel of the spiritual experience of humankind.

As a result, the universal phenomenon is not the anti-Semitism due to social circumstances, as Jean-Paul Sartre thought. But it is the Bible, read as God's Word, which perpetually offers the Jewish people and its story as the access to the holy history in which each and every nation is called to participate through and with Christ.

This is why, as I told you a few minutes ago, whenever and wherever a Bible is opened, even if there are no Jews around, the Jews will be talked about.

However, this means that the nations consider theirs a Word that previously did not belong to them. The question then is, How do they consider those whom the Bible itself calls the Hebrews, the children of Abraham, the sons of Jacob, the people of Israel, the Jews?

♦

But perhaps a parenthetical comment should be made here, because some lexical fine-tuning seems required. According to the biblical vocabulary to which today's Jews remain faithful, there are two categories or groups of human beings: on the one hand the people of Israel, and on the other hand indistinctly all the nations, the goyim.

Let us first emphasize that this differentiation does not correspond to the patterns that ethnologists usually come across. Each tribe or people sees itself as *the* civilized nation, or as the only truly *human* society. This is what the Indians, for example, are reported to have said when speaking of themselves, which implied that others may not have been really human. Likewise, the Greeks used to call all non-Greeks "barbarians."

In contrast, from a Jewish point of view, the distinction is fundamentally religious, not ethnic or cultural. For the nations may become the people of God, provided they share in the covenant. They may abide by its laws and benefit from its blessings.

Judaism has never been very much inclined to practice what is known as proselytizing, even if, during a few decades just before and after Christ, many pagans felt attracted to Judaism and were called "proselytes."

What remains is that today, in the Jewish terminology, the word goyim does not mark out only the pagans but Christians as well. No matter whether they read the Bible as the Word of God or not, all non-Jews are called pagans. Yet, are all Christians goyim? And are all goyim Christians? Is there no difference between them? If so, this would amount to overlooking a basic distinction, and the significance of the divine election.

Christians totally accept the Hebrew Scripture and read it as God's Word. It is not the same with the nations that do not worship the eternal God. For example, consider the Islamic peoples. Even though they do take some biblical elements into account, they have reinterpreted, relativized, and altered them. In like manner, the non-Christian cultures, and especially in Asia, generally fail to find the living God in the Bible and rather tend to see it confusedly as one part of the cultural patrimony of the West.

On the contrary, Christians—whatever their denomination—cannot question, repudiate, or ignore the Hebrew Bible without mutilating their own faith.

Is there then any reason to consider Christians illegitimate possessors? I do not think so. There is no more reason to claim that the Africans or Arabs whose second mother tongue is now French are improperly using a language that they have illicitly borrowed, or to claim that it is illegal to speak English in this country.

It might be fruitful, from the Jewish perspective, to make a clear distinction in favor of those whose faith includes accepting the Hebrew Bible as the Holy Scripture. These believers simply cannot be considered mere plunderers! Not any more can they be branded idolators.

♦

The next question, however, is whether the Bible might not have then become a universal cultural product—some kind of a wonderfully flexible mythology that the various civilizations can refashion according to the needs of the time and place. The great myths of ancient Greece and Rome did play such a complacent and useful role during the last fifteen centuries of Western history.

But the Bible is definitely not this kind of material, no matter whether it is read by Christians or Jews. It is being transmitted, accepted, proclaimed, and meditated upon by successive generations of believers who accept it as the Word of God himself, revealing his mystery and the destiny of humankind. It conveys much more than a myth. This is why this text has an uncommon actual and operative strength, with which the mythologies of the past or Carl S. Jung's archetypes certainly cannot compare. It is a spiritual power, the power of the Holy Spirit, that is continuously at work in human freedom and intelligence, gathering all men and women into a common holy history.

I must repeat that any non-Jew who receives the Bible as God's Word cannot but form an idea of the Jews, even if he or she has never met a Jew, even if he or she will never meet any. It was the case, for instance, with the peoples of Africa or Asia who came to discover the Bible through the Christians, and only by chance actually came across any Jews. And it must be kept in mind that the Bible has reached far beyond the officially Christian regions of the globe.

It then becomes clear that the Jewish vocation, with its history and the conditions resulting from it, is a reality that in its very specificity now has *universal* relevance. Moreover, the Jewish vocation is not a mere cultural item, but it is substantiated by the faith of all the believers, both Jews and Christians, whose lives hinge upon it.

The biblical story is imprinted in the Christian memory. It is part of humankind's treasure. And the image of the Jewish vocation cannot be erased from the experience of the nations.

♦

It must be granted that anti-Semitism does exist and has indeed appeared under various forms. The word itself is fairly recent, and its contents and connotations are mostly secular and often racial. But Jewish history—including the books of Esther and the Maccabees, and extending from Israel's struggle against the pagan empires that surrounded it to its confrontation with the Christian nations—the whole Jewish past cannot be interpreted through the racist and totalitarian theories of the twentieth century.

This is a point that I have said I would not tackle directly: there used to be a Christian anti-Judaism that was based on so-called theological justifications. It led to hatred of the Jews and to charging them with the crime of "deicide." Pope John XXIII and the Second Vatican Council strongly, unambiguously, and solemnly declared that this theory was false and utterly groundless.

Despite this, the Christian tradition's extremely violent indictments of Judaism have not simply disappeared from the works of numerous noted ancient authors—for example, St. John Chrysostom or Martin Luther.

But it would be a serious misjudgment to reduce the image or perception of the Jews or of Judaism to such anti-Judaic or (later) anti-Semitic feelings. Even if this resentment has had tragic and bloody effects, even if the Jewish experience is still deeply and lastingly wounded, the course of world history will inevitably fail to make any sense if the grace that I am recalling is overlooked. That is, the image of the Jew and of Judaism, which is given in the Bible and which Christians have never forgotten, is much more complex, pregnant, diversified, and positive. Reducing everything to anti-Semitism amounts to locking oneself up in a siege position. It also amounts to smothering human hope.

Anyway, the key issue remains, How did the nations and peoples who became Christian understand and accept the first covenant, or the Old Testament?

It should be plain that the disciples of Jesus were enlightened by their faith and, consequently, that they received and interpreted the revealed document in a Christian or messianic perspective. Here, the word "messianic" is to be taken in its etymological sense, that is to say, with a precisely determined historical significance, since these Christians acknowledged and believed that Jesus of Nazareth was the Messiah. The Christian faith, as passed on to us by the writings of the New Testament, is but the development of what is already implied in the statement "Jesus is Christ," or "Jesus is the Messiah."

Some people, Jewish or not, may object that they do not share the Christian faith. But can these people claim to be indifferent to the way Christians understand the Hebrew Bible? What is actually at stake with the reception of the Bible is the way Christians of all nations discover the existence of the people of Israel, its vocation, its destiny, and the share that they themselves can take in its story. Preaching to the pagans precisely consists in telling them that, thanks to Christ the Messiah, they are graciously offered the possibility to participate in the covenant, by uniting with God's anointed who has overcome death and gives access to the one Creator and Father of all human beings.

This is what the Roman Catholic liturgy expresses during the Easter Vigil—the Jewish Passover celebrated by Jesus while offering himself in his death and resurrection. Here is the prayer that follows the reading of the sacrifice of Abraham of Genesis, chapter 22:

> Most Holy God, Father of all believers, by spreading the grace of adoption, you multiply the children of your Promise all around the world. In the Easter mystery, your servant Abraham becomes, as you had promised, the father of all nations.

Another prayer says: "Give all humans the faith that may allow them to participate in Israel's privilege and be regenerated by receiving your Holy Spirit."

Many other liturgical prayers could be quoted. What I want to emphasize is that these prayers express the very substance of Christian belief. According to the striking ancient formula, *Lex orandi, Lex credendi*—the law of prayer is the law of belief.

Now, all these expressions of faith do not evoke any kind of a "supersessionism." The point is absolutely not to eliminate Israel and replace it with another people. It is rather to give all nations access to what was announced and contained in the promise made to Abraham and the irrevocable gift made to Israel (see the Epistle to the Romans 11:29).

There is an objection that some of you may already have in mind: it is the notion of the supersession of the people of Israel in favor of Christians, because the former is supposed to have been rejected on account of its refusal to recognize the Messiah. This accusation has certainly been a source of enmity against Jews in Christian history. It is a distressing problem, full of agony and darkness. I have chosen not to grapple with it today, because I wish to dwell upon another aspect that this difficulty has often obscured and concealed.

♦

From a Christian viewpoint, the New Testament consists of writings which are added to the biblical documents. They have the same authority because they are the products of the same inspiration. Yet, they are, in a sense, of a different nature. For the texts of the New Testament are centered on the person of the Messiah, his predication, his action, and his relationship with what precedes— that is, the people of Israel and the Scriptures that reveal its vocation and destiny, the promise and the covenant. The New Testament proclaims that the Messiah has carried out his mission. With the gift of the Holy Spirit, he plays the central role in human history until the end of time. Christians hope for the glorious return of the Messiah for the final judgment of all resurrected human beings.

As a result, the New Testament is Holy Scripture. But it could be said that it is also the sacrament of God's glory, whereas the Hebrew Bible is both the prophecy of this glory and its memorial.

♦

I am fully aware that there is another widespread objection. It is what Professor Yeshayahu Leibovitz repeated recently in an interview with the Parisian evening daily *Le Monde* of last October 13. I quote:

The need for a Jewish-Christian dialogue is felt on the Christian side only. For Christians, the stubborn existence of Judaism is unacceptable, since Christianity presents itself as the true Israel, in other words as the inheritor of Judaism—and no one can inherit from a person who is not dead. On the other hand, for Jews, the existence of Christianity makes no difference. From our point of view, the Christian faith is but one of the available means to reject the *Halakhah*. This is the reason why no genuine dialogue is actually thinkable between Judaism and Christianity as religions—even if, at a strictly human level, personal dialogue always remains possible between individual Jews and Christians.

I wish to express my most respectful but determined disagreement with the two points made in this assertion.

First, the notion of the *verus Israel* was studied by Professor Marcel Simon more than half a century ago. It may imply the possible disappearance of the people of Israel, or at least justify contempt. But then the Christian faith itself is wounded. Anyway, this notion cannot express the Christians' relationships to their Jewish roots. The opposition between true and false is purely based on antagonisms and finally proves inadequate because it rules out any continuity or resemblance. It works on the patterns of the murder of the father, or of the repudiation of the elder son. But this is an insult to the heavenly Father.

The metaphor provided by St. Paul in his Epistle to the Romans is that of a grafting, or that of a plant with a stem and branches. It would be quite absurd to assume that the branches can survive if they are cut off from the roots.

It must at least be acknowledged that, to describe the relationship between the messianic people composed of both Jews and pagans, the New Testament offers a rich semantic variety of symbols that definitely transcends all antagonisms.

Second, claiming that Judaism has no reason to become interested in Christianity as a religion is an opinion that history does not confirm.

Everything depends on what is meant by Judaism. Should it define itself by ignoring Christianity, then it would lock itself up and fail to acknowledge the fecundity that has been given from on high to the Jewish people and its election in the history of humankind. Without resorting to philosophical or theological arguments, may I limit myself to a cultural comparison? Let us go back to the question of languages. What would we think of the inhabitants of the British Isles if they decided that the legitimate Anglo-Saxon heritage had nothing to do with, and should expect nothing from, the Americans and other English-speaking peoples in Asia and Africa?

♦

Martin Buber dealt with the relationship between Judaism and Christianity in his book, *Two Types of Belief: The Christian and Jewish Faiths*. He finished it 1943. It was published in German in 1950, under the title *Zwei Glaubenweisen*, and was only recently translated into French. Martin Buber offers a heuristic distinction between the Jewish *emuna* and the Christian *pistis*. He sees them as two modes of belief that constantly influence each other. His often mentioned characterization of Judaism as the "Elder Brother" is perhaps the most striking feature of a reflection that is the work of a philologist as well as historian of religions. The Jewish *emuna* refers to the history of a people, and the Christian *pistis* implies the story of an individual. *Emuna* is trust and perseverance, while *pistis* involves a cognitive logic.

Buber explains:

> If Israel strove to renew its faith by breathing new life into the human person, and if Christianity strove to renew its faith by breathing new life into peoples, they would both have many untold things to tell each other, and they would become able to help each other, which is hardly imaginable today.

What I would like now is to provide a very modest contribution to fulfill Martin Buber's wish. I consider him not only as one of the most distinguished minds in our century, but also as one of the men who have grasped best the uniqueness of the Jewish and Christian faiths.

♦

Let me try to illustrate what I have in mind with an example, so as to bring out the figure of Israel as it is reflected in Christian eyes when they are faithful to the grace that opens them up and receive the light of Holy Scripture.

The first page of the Bible describes the divine creative act. The book in which the very existence of the people of Israel is rooted thus begins with the most universal statement that can be thought of. Unlike the pagan myths, which usually report the birth of a tribe or ethnic group through the story of a founding father, the Bible does not begin by telling about the origin of the first Jew. On the contrary, the singularity of Israel as a people stands out against a universal background, since the whole story gets under way as the history of humankind—or, to be more precise, as a reminder of the human vocation, with the fundamental choices and the spiritual and moral options that condition the growth of humankind and fashion its existence.

The very first pages of the book of Genesis thus tell a story of really historic proportions. It is the same with the tale of Noah, who can be hailed as the second father of all humans, as God's power saves him from being swept away by the destructive flood that has been swollen by sin.

When the promise and the covenant take shape with Abraham, from the start the singularity of the election and the gift of having descendants are linked to the service of humankind as a whole. "All the nations of the earth shall be blessed in him," as we can read in Genesis 18:18—*Kol goyié ha'aretz.*

The promise made to Abraham and Abraham's election were thus oriented towards a universal blessing. This correlation between the singularity and the universality of grace is characteristic of the whole biblical tradition.

It is the same generous logic of the particular and the universal that shapes Christian historical awareness, which is rooted, from the very first pages of the Bible, in the story of a specific and irrevocable election. This way of thinking characterizes the biblical revelation of the one God, may he be blessed. His gifts are always particular—for the universal good of all humans.

As a result, the history of Israel keeps on oscillating between two poles, and the tension between them suggests the spiritual stakes: On the one hand the fulfillment of the promise which constitutes the people in its singularity, with all the blessings accompanying the faithfulness that God expects from his chosen people. And on the other hand Israel's vocation to serve all the nations and share with them the gifts that it has received.

◆

Another remark has to be added here. It is that Israel's uniqueness consists essentially in learning about the one true God who liberates his people from bondage—and fundamentally from enslavement to idols. If the nature of slavery in Egypt is social and economic, it is also spiritual, because the descendants of Jacob are prevented from answering the call to serve God and no one else.

When, according to the book of Exodus (5:1), Moses tells Pharaoh in the name of God, "Let my people go!" this is generally considered an affirmation of the national identity of the people of Israel. But the end of the sentence is then omitted. If the people of Israel are to leave Egypt, it is "so that they may celebrate a festival to me in the wilderness" (see also Exod 7:16). A little further (Exod 12:38), the Bible tells us that the people that had thus been gathered was "a mixed crowd." It is thanks to God's call, and to the mission it is given to worship the one true God in the name of all nations, that the people receives its unity and identity. Worship is thus the source of its liberation, and also restores its human dignity.

As a result, Israel's particularity is in the liberation that is *graciously* granted. If the people of Israel have been released from bondage, it is not because God has bestowed a privilege. It is a grace, a gratuitous gift, a token of the love that God wants to extend to all human beings. So, what differentiates Israel from the nations is that it is called to bear witness to the universal vocation of whole humankind, while already enjoying the deliverance that God offers to all.

In contrast, human cultures traditionally distinguish one group from another on the basis of ethnic, physical, social, or linguistic characteristics—that is, on the basis of anything that reflects the diversity and divisions of humankind, using criteria that are genetically or culturally transmissible and that refer to heredity, language, or customs.

One consequence of this is that any notion of nationalism or racism—to borrow the contemporary terminology that could not be found in the Bible—is unthinkable in the biblical perspective. As described by the Bible, Israel's relationship with its land is an example for all nations. Israel's vocation thus illuminates the relationship of each nation with its own land. The question is, Who is the possessor of the land—God or the people? Is the nation literally the landlord, or is the land entrusted to the people by the Lord God? And what does such a trust require? This is the question that each nation must face. The choice of one people, which has been rescued from idolatry so as to become able to worship the one, true, and living God, simultaneously gives this people the mission to bear witness to all the nations that are still suffering enslavement to idolatry.

Christianity is based on "the fulfillment of God's promises." This teaching is sometimes challenged, although it comes straight from the Bible. If Jesus Christ our Lord is the Messiah, it means that God's promise in the Bible of a universal salvation is being fulfilled, with all nations being called to commune in grace and love.

When St. Paul says in the Epistle to the Galatians, chapter 3, verse 28, that there is no longer "Jew or Greek," or nations, that is, goyim, and there is no longer "slave or free, there is no longer male and female," his words simply foretell the final achievement of the history of humankind. And this also characterizes the destiny of the people of God, the gift that gathers it, and the vocation that allows its existence.

Two different approaches of history are then possible. Either the role of the Elder Brother, the Jewish people, is acknowledged; or the nations remain desperately in search of themselves. Christians are thus confronted with a spiritual choice that is not always without political consequences. Either their memory and their hope for the salvation of all help them recognize in human history the first stones of God's city, with Israel and Jerusalem as its perennial symbols, or the nations will lock themselves up in self-love, division, and disunion, while scorning the almighty God and his providential plan for humankind.

Because of their pagan traditions, the heathen nations, even if they have become Christian, are going to be tempted to seize the divine gift for themselves and to translate the share they receive in the election into ethnic and nationalistic terms. This temptation will be all the stronger as the biblical and Christian hope is converted back into pagan ambitions. This is the temptation against which the prophets worked to warn Israel.

The notion of the election then risks being reduced to a national or purely political messianism, and the original biblical universalism may be perverted into imperialistic greed. One nation may claim to be the chosen people that is superior to all the others and has the right and duty to assimilate or annihilate them.

What then happens to the people of Israel? From the eighteenth century on, this same notion that has haunted the will to power of the great nations of the West was projected on the Jews themselves. They were accused of striving to conquer and dominate the world. The initial universality of the Jewish vocation was thus reinterpreted through the pagan impulses that dwell in the hearts of the other nations. These are frightening but, as we know, actual temptations in the moral life of humankind.

But this means that the Christian mission has not been fully carried out yet. It consists in introducing into the particular characteristics of each culture, people, and state, a truly Catholic principle, a longing for universality that is respectful of all differences and opens each nation to the communion with all the others. This does not mean that the various national identities are to disappear, but that they have to be opened to a greater common good.

How then could Christians fail to discover their own vocation when they understand the mission given to the Jewish people?

And how could the Jewish people fail to recognize a confirmation of its own vocation in the mission given to Christians?

♦

Two historical examples may serve to conclude these reflections. The first—a negative one—concerns an ancient feature from the history of France: until the Revolution, France borrowed the notion of its destiny from the story of Israel. This is what has recently been highlighted by a remarkable exhibition at the National Library in Paris. The subject was the Bible in the France of the *ancien régime*. The title was most significant: "God in His Kingdom." Let me quote Emmanuel Leroy Ladurie, who is the curator of the National Library and also a noted historian, in his presentation of this exhibition:

> At the same time, that is, in the thirteenth century, a new ideological theme appears in the writings of the apologists of the royal power: the history of the French and their kings is said to be biblical in essence. France is the "New Israel." A Covenant has been entered into with God after the conversion of Clovis, whose heirs are now hailed as "most Christian sovereigns," and even supposed to descend directly from King David. The statues of the twenty-one kings of Judah on the front of the Cathedral of Notre-Dame in Paris were thus declared in the thirteenth century to portray the French kings.

As far as I am concerned, I cannot but see here an almost perfect example of supersessionism, in the nationalist, not religious, sphere. The election of Israel was similarly misappropriated by the German nation, when one could read: *Gott mit uns*—God with us—on the belt-buckles of the Wehrmacht soldiers. The same could also be noticed about a certain Russian Messianism and its resulting anti-Semitism, based on the idea that only one people may carry out God's mission. In this respect, see the book by David Goldstein, entitled *Dostoevsky and the Jews*, published in France in 1976.

The second, and more positive, example concerns the lot of Black Africans in the New World. This will allow me to justify once more the title I gave for this lecture: "Let My People Go." The African slaves had been deported to the Americas and stripped of their culture. But they had received the Christian faith and, when they needed a cultural expression of their plight, they deliberately chose to identify their condition with that of the Jewish people in Egypt. This is what the famous negro spiritual tells us. This is also how the African Americans managed to survive.

If they eventually won their emancipation, it was thanks to this identification that the Christian faith had made possible. If they had not been evangelized, they would not have received the Old Testament, or they would not have read it as they did. What they found in the Bible was not only the phrases and the metaphors to convey their experience of servitude, but also the words that could give shape to their hope and restore their future. They found in the Bible the strength to struggle for their God-given rights.

Their faith was thus the source of their liberation. In a way, by becoming Christians, they considered themselves as *Bene Israel*, children of Israel. And this may partly explain why American Jews and African Americans have had so much in common for so long.

◆

How would Martin Buber react today, when seeing our world, when recording all the steps that have been made backwards as well as forwards in Christian-Jewish relationships? No one can speak up in his place. But let me quote him again:

> If Israel strove to renew its faith by breathing new life into the human person, and if Christianity strove to renew its faith by breathing new life into peoples, they would both have many untold things to tell each other, and they would become able to help each other, which is hardly imaginable today.

I have only this to add: have we been imaginative enough?

5
Christianity and Religions

An address delivered by Cardinal Lustiger on April 8, 1994, at the Chicago Club, Chicago, Illinois, on the occasion of the inauguration of Reverend John J. Piderit, SJ, as the 22nd president, Loyola University Chicago. Translated by Jean Duchesne.

Reverend President, Most Reverend Fathers, Dear Brothers and Sisters, Ladies and Gentlemen,

I am still moved after yesterday evening's gathering around the Holy Father, in the huge auditorium at the Vatican, of men and women whom it previously seemed impossible to bring together: Jewish survivors of the death camps, leaders of Jewish organizations, all the cardinals present in Rome, and numerous bishops and Christians.

In the morning, the Pope had received former deportees. Many of them had become American citizens, but most spoke Polish with the Holy Father. There was deep, intense emotion.

The evening concert, directed by American maestro Gilbert Levine, began with the recitation of *Kol Nidrei*, and also included a Kaddish.[1]

In truth, this was almost certainly the beginning of a new era, and I remain under the impression that this event casts a bright, fresh light on the subject I propose to deal with here in Chicago: "Christianity and Religions" or "Is religious diversity linked to cultural diversity? And, if it is, can Christianity claim universal relevance?"

I would like to tackle this issue as concretely as possible. The United States can be seen as an impressive conglomerate of religions and cultures. The American civilization is the most exciting place of mutual exchanges in the whole history of humankind. This—let me call it "interculturality"—does not simply mean, however, a cultural plurality where the various cultures would coexist side by side. It is rather an exchange where every one continues to be himself without remaining exactly the same. There are mutual contributions through which the originality of each culture is respected, but also enriched, by its relationships with the others. Here, in the United States of America, each distinct cultural identity asserts itself together with the others and no single one remains foreign. The rule of social integration is based on mutual recognition, and in the course of history itself, this has stimulated a common determination to make up one nation: *E pluribus unum*—one out of many.

THE NATURE OF THE PROBLEM: CULTURAL DIVERSITY AND CHRISTIAN UNIVERSALITY

You all know by experience what is at stake here, and anyone can perceive that two main trends, apparently conflicting, are present in contemporary history.

On the one hand, scientific rationality and technology have spread so much that they tend to govern the thoughts and activities of all human beings on all continents. The universal claim of this rational undertaking is linked to a political universalism, which may be symbolized by the Universal Declaration of Human Rights and also by the establishment of new democracies all around the planet.

But at the same time another, opposite, fact must be acknowledged: the persistent distinctiveness of the great cultures, which are often associated with specific languages, or sometimes with definite geographical areas, while coinciding with institutionalized religions. Even if the notions are jumbled, Christianity appears as the religion of the West—or rather, the Christian religion is still identified with Western culture. This is why the characteristic dynamism of Christianity, consisting of missions and evangelization, remains so easily tied to colonization. Likewise, Islam has been linked to Arabic culture, even though Asian Muslims are much more numerous. In the same way, Hinduism seems to be bound to the Indian culture, and Shintoism to the Japanese culture.

It is almost impossible to foresee the outcome of this conflict between the universalism of modern rationality, and the national, linguistic, religious diversity of the great cultures. The major cultural and religious groups may seem bound to confront each other so as to secure not only their own survival, but also perhaps a supremacy.

However, when distinct cultures assert their uniqueness and demand their autonomy, one suspicion may well arise: does this not imply that the abstract universalism of science, democracy, and economic free trade is but a lie? The ideal of reason and enlightenment might be but the disguise of Western hegemony and even possibly of Christian domination. The Universal Declaration of Human Rights is not universally accepted, in fact. The huge nation of China still rejects the notion of human rights, while acknowledging only two other aspects of Western universalism: technology and the logic of economic profit. This is only one example. You can think of many others.

The point is that a shift has taken place in the last few years. We used to think that rational universalism simply had to overcome the most archaic obstructions, but we now have to face the notion that the universalism born in the West threatens the various other cultures and religions of the earth.

In the resulting confusion, some people hope to find a way by organizing a kind of "religious melting pot," since they have failed to promote exchanges between the cultures and the nations. What I call "religious melting pot" is the temptation to mix up everything, the drift toward syncretism that can be detected both in the West and in the East.

In reality, the tension between rational universalism and the various religions and cultures is a product of the history of the West. It was within the Christian tradition that culture and society on the one hand, and religion and faith on the other hand, were first distinguished, then separated, and later sometimes opposed. In other eras and places of human history, religion and culture are so closely linked that they are almost synonymous with one another.

This remark may help us to understand where Western universalism actually comes from and what it truly means. The universal relevance of rationality merely echoes and reflects the revelation of the truth of the one God. If the believer is to bear the suspicion of the charge of "imperialism," he need only recall the hope given to all by the Gospel: by proclaiming that brotherhood has been promised from on high to all nations, he answers the objections and accusations that may undermine the church's missionary impulse.

Let us keep this in mind when dealing with the question of Christian universality across cultural diversity. I said I wished to tackle the issue as concretely as possible. Now "concretely" also means "within history," that is to say, we have to take into account the history of revelation. The history of salvation requires our faith, which is the root of our religions. Our faith illuminates the process through which our civilization took shape; it unveils its capacities for exchanges and communion.

So let us open the Bible and meditate once more upon the decisive events of the revelation on Mount Sinai and the birth of the people chosen by God.

I. The Revelation of God and the Paradoxical Condition of Israel

By revealing himself, the one God liberates and sets up a people to worship and serve him. This election includes the following paradox: it is that the Lord God of Israel is the God of all peoples. The one true God is the God of all nations, whose divinities may be superior to man but are nothing, worthless, useless fantasies, mere idols when compared to him. The biblical faith makes it clear: the almighty Lord God of Israel, the one true God, wants to save all human beings. The whole of humankind makes up but one family, created by God in his image and resemblance. One day, he will reveal himself to all. One day all nations and all cultures will be united and will share, as a single people, the life of their sole

Creator and Father. The hope of salvation for all is contained in the promise made to one. God will do for all what he once did for Israel when he liberated it from Egypt. There will be another Passover and another Exodus—for all nations. Together with the uniqueness of God, this shared hope is the root of what must be called—and this is no anachronism—the catholicity of the kingdom to come.

In the meantime, the revelation of God to and through one people among others remains an astonishing paradox. What is so special about this people? Is it its culture? Yes, it is, in a way—albeit in a very unusual sense when compared to the rich and powerful civilizations among which this people found its place.

The originality of this people consists in the uniqueness of revelation and of the faith it requires. This is a people called to become holy in order to manifest God's holiness to all people. The essence of this calling is that a "stiff-necked" people is turned into a sacerdotal nation. In its reality as a people, as a body, Israel thus becomes the "priest" of the one God, a priest for all nations (Exod 19:5–6; Isa 43:20–21; cf. 1 Pet 2:9–10).

This people is unlike any other nation, even if it strives to become like all the others and expects to receive similar institutions—for example a king—from God himself. Its paradoxical *specificity* is thus to be the messenger of *universal* hope. In its cultural specificity—or rather, its cultural uniqueness—the chosen people is a prophet for all the other peoples on earth. It announces what all may hope for, and what every one is called to, by the God whom they may not know, but who has created them.

A sinful nation thus receives as a gift from God the law where all the intuitions of humankind's moral, spiritual, and religious conscience can be found. And this nation can thus be expected to waste no time in doing all the good that any man aspires to.

Such is the paradox of God's lightning presence at one moment of human history: God revealing himself within a culture that is condensed in the existential belief and the confession of the faith of one people. Among the monumental civilizations of antiquity, there was no other Hebraic culture than that of a religious language, used to worship the Creator and remember his Torah.

The existence of Israel proved to be even more of an enigma when the faith and the very survival of this people were challenged by great empires with universal claims. The Greek and Roman empires, based on reason and law, carried the seeds of today's imperialisms, even though they remained but rough drafts. Their ambitions were only distant forerunners of the power and limitless aspirations of universal modernity.

Another force, another spirit, another instrumental determination were needed. This was the fight of the Messiah against the idols. It has cut through, torn open, and widened the heart of every man, whether Jewish or pagan, as Saint Paul says. Yes, the originality of sacred history is the true source of modern universalism.

II. The Sacerdotal People and the Salvation of All Nations

1. God's People among the Nations

The struggle first opposed the people of Israel and the great pagan empires. The domination of Antiochus Epiphanes was followed by that of the Romans, whose *Imperium* went unchallenged after the two Jewish wars of AD 70 and 130. The heroes of the Maccabean rebellion have since epitomized martyrdom in the Jewish, and then Christian, memories.

After those persecutions, the Jewish people were dispersed, and its existence has since become encapsulated in its call and mission, condensing itself in the study of revelation. As a witness among the nations of the Lord God of all nations, in the middle of most diversified cultures, this sacerdotal people has focused on the service of the Word to which it owes even its worldly existence.

This uniqueness was the cause of many persecutions. As Haman had already said to King Ahasuerus, "There is a certain people scattered and separated among the peoples in all the provinces of your kingdom; their laws are different from those of every other people..." (Esth 3:8).

2. *The Spiritual Struggle: "The Son Sets You Free" (John 8:36)*

However, in the meantime the battlefield had moved into the invisible realm of hearts and minds. It no longer was resistance to the pagan idols only, as it had also become a fight against the idolatry that strikes at the hearts of the faithful.

Another aspect of the uniqueness given to Israel is then that both the inside and the outside of things are proffered together in one revelation. This is what Jesus teaches in his criticism of those who clean only the outside of the cup: "First clean the inside of the cup, so that the outside also may become clean" (Matt 23:26).

As soon as the law of holiness is given, happiness depends on an obedient heart. As Saint Paul says (Gal 3:24), the law is the teacher opening the sinner's eyes to the depth of the mystery, by making him fathom the abyss from which he is calling—"Out of the depths I cry to you, O Lord" (Ps 130:1)—while showing him the way to salvation:

> Sacrifice and offering you do not desire,
>> but you have given me an open ear.
> Burnt offering and sin offering
>> you have not required
> Then I said, "Here I am;
>> in the scroll of the book it is written of me.
> I delight to do your will, O my God;
>> your law is within my heart" (Psalm 40:6–8).

The revelation of the true sacrifice is imprinted in Israel's memory with the words of the prophet Isaiah: "He has borne our infirmities and carried our diseases.…he was wounded for our transgressions, crushed for our iniquities; upon him was the punishment that made us whole, and by his bruises we are healed.…he was oppressed, and he was afflicted, yet he did not open his mouth" (Isa 53:4, 5, 7).

In his preaching, Jesus the Messiah does not comment upon this prophecy of the suffering servant. He simply accomplishes it in his obedience, through which he receives and transmits the salvation promised by God. This is carried out in his loneliness, first at Gethsemane—"Father...not my will but yours be done" (Luke 22:42)—then on Golgotha "Father, into your hands I commend my spirit" (Luke 23:46).

At that time, the people might think there were no more prophets. But the perfect obedience of Jesus is the highest of all prophecies, as he accomplishes them all in his mortal flesh where the splendor of the eternal Word is revealed. After the disciples had received from the risen Lord the light of the Holy Spirit, they discovered what glory was already shining on the cross.

The beloved Son prophetically exposes the idols, even inside the consciences of the faithful. As he goes as far as the cross to share God's unlimited mercy for the sinners, he makes them realize that their sins come from idolatry, from the false gods that they serve in the secret of their hearts. The meek, humble, crucified Jesus attracts all people. He calls them to holiness, so that they may be set free from their idols and fulfill their vocation to be the priests who worship in spirit and in truth (John 4:24).

3. "Make Disciples of All Nations" (Matt 28:19)

The liberation by Christ's grace from the idolatry of the heart opens human minds to the one, living, and true God. Man thus becomes capable of remaining faithful to God's love. The spiritual fight for truth and love is won by no other than the Son of man. Thanks to him only, God's design to abolish the fences that separate human beings and their cultures can be accomplished.

The communion made possible by the Prince of Peace has its root in the grace given to Israel. The very nature of the struggle and of the victory of the Messiah is transfigured. It is no longer nation against nation, or culture against culture. It is not even the one, true, and living God against the idols of the nations, who have stopped their ears and shut their eyes, so that they might not see with their eyes nor listen with their ears (cf. Isa 6:9–10). The fight for spiritual freedom is fought in reconciled hearts. The Spirit of the Messiah has engraved this in every person's conscience, so that the idols that enslave may be unmasked and crushed into dust.

As long as humankind exists, the messianic drama is replayed, by every human liberty, at every period, and in every culture where the truth is put to the test.

This means that the nations now share in the unique covenant. As Saint Paul wrote to the Ephesians: "The Gentiles have become fellow heirs, members of the same body, and sharers in the promise in Christ Jesus through the gospel" (Eph 3:6). Jesus had asked, "Make disciples of all the nations" (Matt 28:19). And Paul comments, he "is the Savior of all people" (1 Tim 4:10).

4. The Israel of God and the Time of the Pagans (Cf. Gal 6:16)

In him who is our peace and reconciliation, the vocation of Israel to be a priest for all nations begins to bear fruit through the call of the Gentiles to join the sacerdotal people.

Between them, in their middle, stands the mystery of the suffering Messiah, as both "a sign that will be opposed" (Luke 2:34) and the one who brings about communion. His life is offered for the redemption of all. Through him, the grace of becoming the child of God is offered to each and every human being, until "the fullness of time [has] come" (Gal 4:4). The tension created by this hope enlightens the time we live in, the "time of the nations," until the Messiah comes back in his glory and gathers all humankind in full communion, sharing the life of the children of God.

This time of the pagans is the period when the universality of creation and salvation is materializing. The mystery of God's historic design has not yet been fully unveiled. This is the time of the universal mission that is not yet fulfilled, the time when the spirit of the Messiah is at work in every human being and every culture.

As Father Jean-Miguel Garrigues said recently in one of his Lenten lectures at Notre Dame of Paris:

> The people of Israel and the Church who is, without Israel knowing it, the messianic assembly that integrates the nations into the covenant, walk together in this world along the rugged road of hope in God.

In her martyrdom, the Church is comforted by the Holy Spirit who already gives the Christians, in the obscurity of faith, a taste of "the goodness of the word of God and the powers of the age to come" (Heb 6:5). She knows that this "hope does not disappoint us, because God's love has been poured into our hearts through the Holy Spirit that has been given to us" (Rom 5:5). But she is ceaselessly tempted to mistake herself—or worse, any nation that she has evangelized—for the advent of God's kingdom in history.

On the same road of hope in God's promise, Israel also is progressing to meet its Lord. But it is a progress on which the Passover of the Suffering Servant does not cast the light of His victory over evil and death. This is why Israel's hope is constantly and grievously hurt by hostility and the scandal of evil, especially in our times with the extreme injury and malevolence of the Shoah inflicted upon its very identity. With faithfulness bordering on despair, Israel demands silence over Auschwitz, like Rachel "weeping for her children," she refuses "to be comforted" (Jer 31:15; Matt 2:18).

According to a theological view that is genuinely faithful to the New Testament, the Israel that does not believe that Jesus is the Messiah and the Son of God has not become redundant in this world. In God's design, there is no rivalry between Israel and the Church. But God does demand that both Christians and Jews should acknowledge the ultimate mystery of His plan in history, which has not yet been unveiled....

By its simple existence and its faithfulness to the identity received in its election, Israel reminds the Church that the "time of the nations," the time of her universal mission, is not over. The Church must keep on hoping and carrying her cross of Redemption, while Israel is carrying its own—and no less indispensable—cross, the cross of survival through God's irrevocable election of this people (see Rom 11:28–29). Only in God's supreme victory, in the final Passover of the advent of the Messiah in His glory, will these two crosses become one.

III. The Part of Faith in and Stakes of Cultural Exchanges

1. The People and the Nations

God's revelation was given as a promise and a hope first to Abraham. Later it was given in a series of prodigious wonders when God assembled his people out of Egypt, revealed his name, and entered into the covenant.

Moses received God's commandments so that the people might abide by the law of holiness. This is why Moses, when he saw that the people had reverted to idolatry, cast down the tablets on which God himself had written, shattering them.

But because the people continued to be fashioned by God so that it might give itself to him, God would grant to it a land that his mere presence would make holy. As a token of this gift, this presence would guide the people in its wanderings before finally dwelling in its midst at the temple: "For the Lord has chosen Zion; he has desired it for his habitation: This is my resting place forever; here I will reside, for I have desired it" (Ps 132:13–14).

When the people, because of its infidelity, was deprived of its land and its temple, as well as of its king, its priests, and its prophets, God's plan was not abandoned for a single moment. The Lord wants this people to live as his own people, so that the vocation to which it is called may be accomplished. And the people survived, because the heavenly Father wanted his people to live. It lives thanks to its faith, even though it does not enjoy most of the conditions that the other nations possess. Israel has given itself a culture whose true source is its faith. It is a religious, cultural, and sacerdotal people, rooted in the memory of the revelation. This culture, which is also a religion, has allowed Israel to endure in the most adverse circumstances of its dispersion, but also to actively participate in the cultures and languages of the whole earth.

Such is the uniqueness of a people that is different from all others, because of what has been entrusted to it in order to foster the hope of all.

As far as Christianity is concerned, it has not created any specific culture. Rather, as the famous French historian Henri Irénée Marrou said, it has baptized a great many civilizations. The task of such transformations is being carried on today with the power of the Spirit of the word made flesh.

We should not forget that the one on whom all of revelation is centered, and through whom the Father's plan of salvation is being carried out, is and can be no other than the filial figure of the Messiah. From him, the people taken from all the nations will be born and united to the people from which he had been born. The heritage of Jesus is the whole of creation: "All authority in heaven and on earth has been given to me" (Matt 28:18). His resurrection is open to all the nations—he built the true and eternal temple of God's glory, "the temple of his body" (John 2:21). He has sent the Holy Spirit—through whom God makes the story of his wonders accessible to all the languages of the earth—in "tongues, as of fire" (Acts 2:3).

God's design and human history are concentrated in the person of the humiliated and glorified Messiah. It is then impossible to link him to any one culture among others. He will only promote worship in spirit and in truth. The blessing of all the nations promised to Abraham and his descendants, the law given to Moses so that all may learn, the divine presence intended to welcome all the peoples at the top of the holy mountain—all this is engraved until "these last days" (Heb 1:2) in the "heart of flesh" (cf. Ezek 36:26) of those who know the Father and contribute to the work of salvation, in the meek and humble heart of the Messiah, through him and with him.

The various cultures refashioned by Christianity are marked by the specific genius of the nations that gave birth to them. Yet, each one possesses a Catholic characteristic, and this unites them all across their diversity and ensures their consistency and their communion as the centuries go by. For instance, Coptic-Egyptian Christianity is quite different from the church of the Byzantine

Empire, or from the Hispanic culture of the sixteenth century, which remains so visible in the Latin church....Still, in spite of the variety in languages and customs, aesthetic tastes and sensibilities, the communion continues and overcomes the divisions and the conflicts of history.

Because of the religious originality of its faith, Judaism cannot be reduced to any specific civilization or confused with any of the cultures where it is present. Likewise, Christianity may give way to numerous cultures, but can no more be identified with any of them. On the contrary, it maintains among them and between them the principle of a communion that is rooted in the universal truth of its message, and in the love that constitutes the only hope for the whole world.

Because of the contents of the Christian faith, biblical revelation and tradition thus give a new significance to the term "religion." To be sure, Judaism and Christianity are religions among other religions. But the originality of their faith and the uniqueness of their revelation make their relationships to the various cultures different from those established by other religions, which are more dependent on their circumstantial and political roots.

2. Faith, Religions, and Cultures

The encounter between the biblical revelation and other religions appears extremely complex. A non-biblical religion may allow the stream of living water from the temple to spring in its midst (cf. Ezek 47). It is the water of the gift of the Holy Spirit (cf. John 4:10; 7:38–39). This religion may be renewed and vivified as it sees in a fresh light what it had already received but had been unable to identify. Blaise Pascal's sentence—"You would not look for me if you had not already found me"—is relevant also for all the world's religions. And this is not without consequence for the culture to which they are linked.

There is no denying that culture remains closely bound to religion, as it is bound to the existence of the people whose cohesion it maintains. You cannot grasp the culture of a given people while ignoring its religion. Man is an enigma to himself, because of the transcendence of his vocation. And he exists only in the social life where each person's individual life is given a role and a sense.

But, irresistibly, the image of society comes to be confused with the representation of the divinity, and the latter may even be reduced to the dimensions of the former—unless God reveals himself, sets people free from the idols of the tribe, and invites them to establish new mutual relationships in their link to their Creator. Human cultures are inevitably religious, if revelation does not force them to break away from idolatry. But biblical faith and the worship of the living God are distinct from any cultural exchange.

The worship in spirit and in truth is performed by the Messiah himself in the sacraments and the liturgy of his church, among "a great multitude that no one could count, from every nation, from all tribes and peoples and languages" (Rev 7:9). The *Epistle to Diognetus*[2] describes the Christians as strangers in this world, as pilgrims who claim their right to live inside cultures whose idolatry they still openly reject. The spiritual worship then begets a culture that had so far been foreign, and it also triggers persecutions that may become deadly: "Although they are persecuted, Christians are more and more numerous every day. The mission that God has given them is so noble that they are not allowed to defect."

The distinction between religion and culture becomes apparent here. It is a specific product of the Christian faith. The divine revelation has inserted into human history and religions the presence of his word, made flesh and put to death. This is the source of the greatness of the true religion, that of the worship in spirit and in truth. And this is also the reason why this religion cannot be assimilated to the cultures where it is adopted and practiced. The Christian faith, liturgy, and religion cannot be reduced to the cultures that tap it but that cannot exhaust it. The Christian faith, rather, gives rise to cultures, which it purifies, and whose religious intuitions it reshapes radically. There is no culture that does not need to be transfigured by faith. There is no religion in the world that is not expecting the salvation announced by the Gospel.

The Christian faith has spread as the principle of communion between the descendants of Adam. It was born in the land of Israel, where two thousand years ago Jews and pagans—Asians, Greeks, Africans, Europeans—were already in contact. It took roots all around the Mediterranean Sea, transfiguring the local cultures. It then permeated the various traditions of the so-called barbarians of northern Europe—Celts, Germans, Angles, Saxons and Slavs—not to mention the peoples of the East as far as India. Revelation has found homes among these different nations and is transmitted in their languages. The power of the Holy Spirit is manifested: He arouses faith, purifies religious feelings, enlightens the minds, and liberates the human imagination from its idols. The Gospel was later offered to the Africans, to the Chinese, to the Japanese, to all people all around the world. With such an impetus, the culture of the missionaries may too often have appeared domineering. But the spiritual principles that motivated them have been communicated to other peoples, and this has made possible a still broader communion, including even new cultures.

Intercultural exchanges can be the field of merciless struggles, which may end only with the annihilation of a civilization, if the latter is overwhelmed by the conquerors. Yet, another behavior can be observed, and it is probably more widespread than the policy of destructive conquest. At the beginning of this address, I used the term "interculturality" to describe it. In its original significance, this word refers to *agape*—God's charity or love. The cultural diversity of Christianity in its first centuries seems to confirm such an assumption.

CONCLUSION

It should now be easier for us to understand the conflict I referred to initially, opposing Western-born secular universalism to cultural and religious diversity.

Genuine universalism may seem to have in reality two faces. What I call "universalism" is the view that sees humanity not only as the human species, but as the unity of the living and the dead, the communion between persons who are entrusted to the same memory and to a common hope.

First, humanity is one and indivisible because of its common origin. This fundamental unity of humankind justifies the universalist ambition to gather all human beings while respecting their diversity. As the fathers of the last council said in *Nostra Aetate*, "All peoples make up one community. They all have one and the same origin as God has made the human race inhabit the face of the earth. They also have one common final end, that is to say God himself, whose providence, blessings, and redemptive design are extended to all, until the elect are gathered in the holy city luminated by God's glory, with all peoples proceeding in his light." Revelation thus announces the universalism of redemption, in showing the only one God as the Savior of his whole creation.

Secondly, as humanity is defined through God's splendor and transcendence, it is also revealed to itself. Its greatness is clearly asserted. Human beings can then rightly develop the ambition to use their rationality to refashion the universe that has been entrusted to them. Such an enterprise is not presumptuous in itself. It bears all kinds of fruit: scientific, political, economic, and, as a result, cultural. The strength of reason does not necessarily lead to turning its power into an idol.

The two aspects of universalism that I have just mentioned appeared chronologically in the same order. The universal mission of the revealed religions first became part of the history of human beings and peoples. These religions thus asserted their difference from other religions. Their faith has created a gap that can no longer be bridged between human cultures and true worship. And in the second stage, by introducing hope for all, these revealed religions made possible the emergence of the secular universalism that I briefly characterized at the beginning of this lecture.

Professor Peter Hodgson from Oxford wrote recently about the scientific enterprise that "it was the Christian belief in the creation of the world out of nothing that provided [...] the ideas about the world that formed the foundation of science" (*Christianity and Science*). Despite the tensions between faith and politics, the same should be asserted concerning human rights and the rise of democracies. Human rights, as well as the scientific spirit, were brought about by the Bible and Christianity, in the same way as the tree bears fruit or the child is born from his parents.

The two faces of universalism are not contradictory and rather suggest the unity of humankind, in spite of all the antagonisms. The universality of human reason and the uniqueness of the divine revelation are historically linked. Their common origin accounts for the double purpose that they both share: the service of humanity and the community with God.

The stakes for the future should now become plain. The struggle between the universality of reason and religious or cultural diversity is not likely to come quickly to an end. But a more serious threat lies in the claim of rational universalism to manage human societies while denying their fundamental relationship to the Creator and Savior of all people. The rational project on which a world civilization is being built might become truly satanic. It might impose itself as an absolute and thus enslave man instead of setting him free.

The devastating truth about idolatrous universalism has already been exposed in the preachings and sufferings of the Messiah. Reason will be able to fulfill its mission in history only if it does not repudiate or strive to destroy its divine source. One of the conditions necessary for reason to reach the truth is humility, which points to its limits and recalls its destiny. The natural diversity of humankind must be respected, because it is designed to achieve communion through and with God.

As the late Jesuit Cardinal Jean Daniélou wrote more than forty years ago, "Our duty as Christians is no longer to preach the ambiguous humanisms that are mere collusions with the idolatry of these times. It is to recall that only God is God, and that all that is being built without God is doomed and will be consumed in the fire of judgment" (*Dieu vivant* 20, 1951)—that is, unless we faithfully bear witness to the hope for the salvation of this world (John 3:17).

Thank you for your attention.

6
The Uniqueness of the Shoah, an Homage to Professor Saul Friedländer

When the German University of Witten awarded an *honoris causa* degree to Professor Saul Friedländer, who teaches history at UCLA and the University of Tel Aviv, Cardinal Lustiger was asked to give an address on July 8, 1997. The French original was published in the January 1998 issue of the Jesuit journal *Etudes*, Paris, pp. 73–79. Translated by Jean Duchesne.

What makes the Shoah unique? When investigating the tragedy of Nazism, Professor Friedländer offered penetrating insights towards an answer to this question. Here are the final lines of his book entitled *Reflections of Nazism*[1]:

> The liberal creed and the Marxist creed imply assurance of salvation by the cumulative acquisition of knowledge and power. Neither liberalism nor Marxism responds to man's archaic fear of the transgression of some limits of knowledge and power (you shall not eat the fruit…), thus hiding what remains the fundamental temptation: the aspiration for total power, which, by definition, is the supreme transgression, the ultimate challenge, the superhuman combat that can be settled only by death.

Linked as it is to a great extent to the rise of modernity, does this vision still run through our imaginations, does it remain a temptation for today and for tomorrow? We know that the dream of total power is always present, though dammed up, repressed by the Law. Also constant is the temptation to break the Law, even at the risk of destruction. With this difference—which perhaps tempers, or on the contrary exacerbates, the apocalyptic dreams: This time, to reach for total power is to assure oneself, and all of mankind as well, of being engulfed in total and irremediable destruction.

In this tribute to Saul Friedländer, I shall not aim at discussing a most remarkable work, based on nearly forty years of research. My purpose will rather be to offer my own modest tentative understanding of the same enigma. These reflections will be based on the biblical experience, where I see a light that may enhance the uniqueness of the Shoah.

WHAT MADE THE SHOAH UNIQUE

This uniqueness is brought into relief by the question, *Whom did the Shoah target, and why?* Of course, not all the victims of the camps were Jewish, and one may well ask whether the universal consciousness allows the Jewish consciousness to claim that the Shoah was tragically unique. Might there not be some selfishness within the agony? Recent debates among historians have tended to downplay this uniqueness, while the "negationists" are striving to get rid of it altogether by contending that it is an imposture. What remains, however, is an indelible silence that suggests unprecedented shame. As Saul Friedländer wrote:

The Nazis themselves didn't keep quiet about the execution of the SA chieftains or their other political "opponents." But one knows that the attitude toward the Jews was not the same. At the time of the final phase—that of massive extermination—the impossible was attempted in order to hide the facts.[2]

As the Nazis saw it, the extermination of the Jews was a sacred mission:

> On October 4, 1943, Heinrich Himmler addressed the SS generals gathered in Posen: "This is a glorious unwritten page of our history, one that will never be written....We had the moral right, we had the duty to our people to annihilate the people who wanted to annihilate us." [Himmler sees the Nazis as] an elite who must accomplish the hardest labors, and, at the same time, keep to [themselves] what [they] alone are fit to understand. [Himmler] undertakes the neutralization of what he is going to say by linking the action he describes—the extermination of the Jewish people—to stable values, to rules everyone acknowledges, to the laws of everyday life. This "cover" has one clear aim: Insert extermination into the fabric of required behavior that is universally accepted, to evacuate its load of horror.[3]

The unintentional confession of such a plan points out the historic spiritual horror of a subversion that casts out, together with Israel, everything that this people mysteriously carries: the divine Word, the law, the commandments, with all that they inescapably mean for the Jewish and Christian cultures founded on faithfulness to these precepts (Matt 5:17–19, 48; Gal 5:14). Against this cultural background, Nazism presents itself as a denial, a negation of God's commandments.

In the Shoah, the witnesses of the law and the author of the law are uniquely disowned through a free decision that the biblical experience identifies as the *sin of man*. In the light of this experience, what the Shoah makes visible on earth is extreme evil, the "the mystery of lawlessness" (2 Thes 2:7), which we can interpret as a sin for the sake of sinning. This causes man to become his own idol by eliminating that very people who bears witness to God's testimony. The Jews, then, must be killed in order to get rid of the commandments of the unique Lord—even if, obviously, not all of the six million victims chose personally to carry out this mission within the tragedy of human history.

THE BLACK LIGHT OF THE SHOAH

But the Shoah is not only unique. Inasmuch as it disowns the witnesses of the Sinai testimony, through them it also rejects the unique one in whom are rooted the freedom and the wisdom of every human conscience. This aversion to the one God reveals to humankind the abyss of evil—the abyss of *every* evil.

Thanks to the "black light" of the Shoah, it becomes possible to call other horrors by their names, those perpetrated in Bosnia, in Rwanda, Pol Pot's crimes in Cambodia, the Armenian genocide, and so many others that are concealed under the deceptive cloak of political motivations. In consequence, a negationism that denies the facts, or a revisionism that "doctors" them, cannot be attributed to skepticism or to the relativity of human opinions, because these attitudes are characteristic of a universal temptation. They are but forms of lie that always deny the truth in order to avoid it.

For all its horrible significance, the Shoah does not make the other wounds of this century any less hideous. Quite the opposite, it shows to the human conscience that the smallest damage to human dignity is unbearable. If one consequence of the Shoah is that any violation of human dignity becomes unacceptable, this is because the plan to exterminate the people of the witness focuses on the condition and vocation of every human person. Beyond the number of the victims, what the planned annihilation of the chosen people reveals is that any crime against humanity is a blasphemy that undermines the integrity of the persons and shatters their communion. Because it is the model of all other exterminations, the Shoah denies the unique God who, with Israel's election for the salvation of all the nations, reveals the link at the heart of history between what is unique and what is universal. When rationality, whose purpose is to serve humankind and the divine communion, becomes the technical tool of extermination, it denies the revelation—given by the unique God—of the plurality of persons and the community of the nations.

This revelation must be recalled here. It has given to our moral law a unique foundation. It has spread this law universally, across the world's cultures and religions. It is expressed, of course, in the Ten Commandments of the Sinai.

THE UNIQUENESS OF THE SINAI

One cannot grasp the uniqueness of the Shoah without referring to the uniqueness of the Sinai. The Shoah is the radical negation of the Sinai. The same features can be found in both these opposite, contradictory, symmetrically contrasted events. The gift of the law is unique and irreversible. The Shoah, which is the negation—or rather the denial—of this gift is no less unique, no less forgettable.

When Hollywood attempted to visualize the Sinai event, Cecil B. DeMille called his film *The Ten Commandments*, and he pictured the well-known scene of God handing out the tablets upon which he had engraved his commandments (Ex 31:18—34:1). It is widely accepted that these commandments reflect the absolute authority of the law, and that the legislator is the personal guarantee of this authority. This intuition received rational strength from the Kantian categorical imperative.

In spite of the relativism and skepticism that can be detected as early as antiquity and even in Blaise Pascal's *Pensées*, it is easy to find this moral treasure, which is the common good of humankind, within the diversity of human customs and cultures. The need to respect one's parents, the institution of marriage, the care for the weak, the regard for the others' possessions, the faithfulness to one's word, the duty to turn to arbitration when necessary—all these show that in all cultures social behavior is based upon a sense of the absolute. This intuition remains valid in modern societies, even though the religious grasp of the sacred has been wiped out of politics and the obligations are routinely defined through majority procedures or according to popular sentiment.

The Ten Commandments and the Sinai are at the unique core of the moral treasure shared by all cultures. The revelation of the unique God traces the unique space where the rejection of the moral law coincides with the extermination of the chosen people.

THE LUMINOUS CLOUD

The self-revelation of the one God, whose name remains mysterious even as he unveils his will, thus gives human beings their dignity and their liberty, while promising them a spiritual destiny. The common conscience of the West and many other nations has assimilated the biblical revelation of the Torah. As a result, morality, insofar as it is linked to religious experience, no longer consists of simply the practice of living in harmony with the sacred powers that build a society and organize the world. It has become a law of sanctity so that human beings may be faithful to their condition as creatures made in God's image and resemblance (Gen 1:27). This is exactly the way the revelation of God's name through the gift of the law has given a specific mission to the people of Israel. This people exists only to glorify God and to offer all humans access to this revelation and participation in the worship "in spirit and truth" (John 4:23).

Since its very birth, Israel has thus been distinguished by two characteristics. It first lives in the uniqueness of the call from the one God to hear and obey in faith the divine Word that makes it a unique people, while also reaching out far beyond that call. Secondly, Israel bears witness to the universality of the moral commandments that characterize it, and the observance of which is entrusted to it as its specific mission. The Sinai revelation summarizes the ethical treasure of all humanity. This is why the extermination of the witnesses of the unique God is, also in this sense, a crime against humanity.

The tension that is at the origin of the people of Israel has always been, throughout its history, at the root of its ordeals. In truth, the Sinai revelation somehow breaks the link between religion on the one hand, and morals and politics on the other hand.

Outside of the biblical revelation, religion usually expresses the sacredness of the cosmos and of social life. The biblical faith can recognize in such religion humanity's quest for the divine, even if this search sinks into idolatry. But the self-revelation of the unique God makes it clear that the absolute is a subject: "I am" (Exod 3:14). Man finds in God, in whose image and resemblance he is created, his absolute origin, which makes of him a person who is called to use his liberty to do what is right, even if this means going against the society where he belongs. In this light, the moral life proves to be an untransferable liberty of the human person, as capable of acknowledging the absolute that judges him. This absolute reveals to the human being the inalienable dignity of his conscience. He can believe in the one in front of whom he is responsible for his acts. Moral life thus becomes the personal fight of liberty to "choose life."

When people want to justify their failing to obey this moral law, they have to ignore the "I am" who is its source and makes it sacred. The creature who claims to have gone beyond good and evil and rebels against the Ten Commandments is tempted to deny the one who gave them. He then has to persecute the witnesses, to reduce them to silence, to eliminate them once and for all. This annihilation of the people of the Torah, this defiance-transgression of the divine Word has led to what Saul Friedländer calls "the paralysis of language."[4]

THE "PARALYSIS OF LANGUAGE"

Friedländer has pointed out that Nazism has produced no literary work that might confront us decisively to the events of its times. On the other hand, Italian fascism, or the Stalinist nightmare, or the capitalist "jungle," or the Germany of before 1933, have all inspired realistic, significant literary achievements.

During the Nazi era, a paralysis struck the language, which could no longer express the reality of the extermination. On the contrary, this reality was hidden beneath the coded phrases and the fallacious jargon of bureaucratic management, progressively depriving the technicians of death of any kind of feeling or interiority.[5]

When Himmler, at the top of a pyramid of dehumanized government officials, justified the extermination of the Jewish people by invoking the love of the German people,[6] he simply confessed—albeit unwittingly—the spiritual depravation of the murderous idolatry that turns a deaf ear to the First Commandment: "You shall have no other gods before me" (Deut 5:7); "You shall love the Lord your God with all your heart, and with all your soul, and with all your might" (Deut 6:5). Here the First Commandment is denied in the name of the idolatry of the race and of all the human sacrifices that this entails.

The divine law transmitted by Israel to the world calls for and invites to the obedience of the heart, through which one day all people, "from the least of them to the greatest" (Jer 31:34), will meet with God. When the Nazi leaders confiscated sense and love, this simply confirmed that the Shoah was nothing but the denial of the Sinai. The paralysis of language and of the heart that were to follow only abandoned man to the power of evil, with the brutal, violent rejection of the divine Word, of its author, and of its witnesses—"for a thousand years, once and for all."

We are always fighting the hardheartedness that the unique and exemplary character of the Shoah exposes deep inside each and every human being. Primo Levi has expressed the shame of Auschwitz, and especially the shame of the guilt for being human since Auschwitz had been built by humans. This spiritual fight is bound to have a heavy cost.

Yet Israel's unique vocation remains ineradicable. This people stays forever as the witness of the revelation of the unique God in human history. The chosen people bears and keeps the hope that one day the Lord will make himself known to all the nations and gather them in the communion of his children.

7
Jews and Christians, Tomorrow

An address by Cardinal Jean-Marie Lustiger on the occasion of his reception of the *Nostra Aetate* Award, Sutton Place Synagogue, New York, October 20, 1998. Translated by Jean Duchesne.

How moving it is for me to be made to feel welcome in this famous and venerable synagogue, already a century old! For this, I am deeply grateful to President Robert Berend and Rabbi Allan Schranz. I also wish to thank for their presence my brother cardinal, Archbishop John O'Connor, and the French consul in New York, the Honorable Richard Duqué.

Needless to say, my gratitude goes especially to Rabbi Joseph Ehrenkranz, Dr. Anthony Cernera, and all the officials of the Center for Christian-Jewish Understanding of Sacred Heart University in Fairfield, Connecticut, and also to Dr. Samuel Pisar for introducing me with such thoughtfulness.

In addition, I wish to thank you all for allowing me to share the *Nostra Aetate* Award with Rabbi René-Samuel Sirat, to whom I feel so close in respect and friendship. His presence here adds to the honor you are doing me. Your selection touches me more than you can imagine. May the Almighty bless your work and efforts.

If such an event can take place here in the United States, there must be a reason. You are all aware of the special conditions that American history and culture have offered to Christian-Jewish relationships, in contrast with Europe and its tragedies. It is my intuition that, for the time being, you are more free than the Christians and Jews of the old continent—where the wounds of the past are still open[1]—to take advantage of all that has been accomplished everywhere in the world, in Europe as well as in Israel.

Next year I will not fail to invite the Catholics of Paris to join the Jewish communities in prayers on Yom Shoah—the Day of the Shoah, April 13, 1999, 27 Nissan 5759—in a spirit of penance and an act of faith in the Lord of the living and the dead. Perhaps this joint prayer service that will take place in Paris can also be done elsewhere, and in particular in New York.

May I go a little further with you now by contemplating the future of the relationships between Jews and Christians? Of course, I cannot erase from my heart and mind all the hardships whose persecutions have been stamped upon the Jewish memory. But I will strive to examine some of these confrontations and interactions, and even some of the contradictory convergences, between Jewish consciousness and Christian consciousness over the last two millennia. For such a clarification is necessary to open a new dialogue that will not merely reproduce the controversies of past centuries.

NEW RELATIONSHIPS BETWEEN JEWS AND CHRISTIANS?

Half a century has passed since the end of the Second World War and the creation of the State of Israel. As we are nearing the third millennium of the Christian era, a new age has begun in the history of humankind. The relationships between Jews and non-Jews have been deeply changed over the last fifty years.

First of all, geographically.

Most of the Jews who had been living—sometimes for more than twenty centuries—in regions that became Islamic countries have returned to Israel or emigrated to lands with a Western, mostly Christian, culture. Furthermore, many Jewish survivors have left Europe and the former Soviet Union, and more are still doing so. One result of all these population movements, which started as early as the end of the nineteenth century, is that no nation, even

Israel, has a greater number of Jewish residents today than the United States. France is the only European country where a comparatively numerous Jewish community has maintained and reconstituted itself thanks to Sephardic immigration from north Africa.

These geographical movements correspond to cultural and spiritual shifts, and also to new types of relationships between Jews and Christians. Europeans are likely to be insufficiently aware of the important work of collating documents that is currently under way within your nation. Most of them still do not know about the encounter between Jewish culture and Christian culture that is taking place in America. This symbiosis is, in part, the successor to that which took place in the former cultural centers of Prague, Warsaw, Vilna, Vienna, Berlin, and so many German university towns, without forgetting Paris and London. America now welcomes Yiddish voices that used to come from the *shtetl* of Poland, Russia, and other East European nations, before the Shoah and the Stalinist purges.

A study of cultural history covering the period from the end of the eighteenth to the end of this century should, of course, show the role played by Jews and Jewish sources in the culture of Western modernity. It should also point out the renewal of Jewish-Christian relationships since 1948, especially in the United States and more especially—this must be acknowledged—here in New York. The fact is that today Jews are respected when living among Western Christians, while the young State of Israel is bordered by Muslim nations.

This radical change in the concrete conditions of Jewish existence is contemporaneous with a very different transformation: the *aggiornamento* intended by the Second Vatican Council for the Catholic Church, inviting her to reach beyond the exclusivism of the old European cultures. The fetters of national feelings and political determinisms had tightened up along the centuries, and for too long they had trapped her spiritual dynamism within the limits of European references.

The tremendous economic and political changes that are taking place today make up the background against which the two upheavals I have evoked stand out—that is, the evolution of the Jewish condition and the renewal of the Catholic Church.[2]

A page is being turned in the history of humankind. Catholics, after all, have only been obeying the words of Jesus when he explained the commandment, *Thou shalt not kill*:

> So when you are offering your gift at the altar, if you remember that your brother or sister has something against you, leave your gift there before the altar and go; first be reconciled to your brother or sister, and then come and offer your gift. (Matt 5:23–24).

If you remember that your brother or sister has something against you. These words in the Gospel do not take into consideration what you think of yourself or the arguments by which you would like to justify yourself or protest of your innocence. They simply acknowledge the other's—your brother's—wound as he, the other—your brother—experiences it.

In Christian-Jewish relationships, Christians have opened their eyes and ears to Jewish pain and hurt. They consent to being held responsible. They agree to bear that burden without shifting it to others. They have not tried to declare themselves innocent. If they have not asked for the victims' forgiveness, it is because they know that only God can grant forgiveness, as the Gospel according to Matthew (9:6) recalls: only God knows what is in man's heart, and he is the only judge. As Jesus also says (Matthew 7:1), "Do not judge" (that is, do not substitute yourself for God), "so that you may not be judged" (that is, so that God will not judge you).

In the name of truth, Christians ask Jews to take part in their examination of conscience. In the French bishops' Declaration of Repentance at Drancy on September 30, 1997, we did not want to insist on the role played by numerous Catholics to save a number of Jews in France. Indeed, this is something that Serge Klarsfeld has brought to light: if there were a good many survivors among French Jews, it is especially—though not exclusively—thanks to Christians, in particular the clergy. Some have reproached the

Drancy Declaration for failing to emphasize this aspect of history. But how could we then have yielded—even unconsciously—to the temptation to justify ourselves?

When the authorities of Yad Vashem instituted the recognition of the "Righteous among the nations," they intended to manifest a concern for the truth in the name of the Jewish people. With a book and a film, Marek Halter also wanted to remember these works of justice. Is this not also the significance of the "French Society to Honor the Righteous among the Nations"? It has been created recently by Mr. Jean Kahn, president of the Central Consistory of France. On November 2nd, 1997, this organization inaugurated at Thonon-les-Bains the "Clearing of the Righteous," in the middle of which a memorial is standing that commemorates the action of the men and women who risked their lives to save thousands of Jews from deportation and death. On the occasion of the inauguration of this memorial, I sent the following message to the participants:

The Righteous remain hidden.

They had to, when between 1940 and 1944 their courage saved thousands of Jews from the death camps.

Today many remain hidden, unknown, or ignored; some of them are forgotten forever.

But their light shines under God's eyes, and warms up the hearts of the survivors who can remember.

I do remember the ones who provided me with forged documents. I do remember those who helped me get across the demarcation line.[3] I do remember those who warned me that I might be arrested soon. I do remember those who put me up without asking any questions. I do remember those whom I trusted and who never betrayed me. I do remember what they did for me in those times of dereliction. Yet I cannot remember their names or sometimes even their faces.

Would I be able to recognize them if they are still alive?

We are moved by the list of those who have been given the title of 'Righteous among the nations.' And we are no less moved when we think of so many unknown people to whom we shall never be able to say thank you.

To perpetuate their memory is a duty for our generation with regard to the next. For the Righteous prove that the best as well as the worst can spring from man's heart.

Such gestures of mutual recognition allow us to examine ourselves more objectively about the ceaseless violence perpetrated against Israel, first by ancient pagan anti-Judaism, then by Christian anti-Judaism with its tragic consequences in medieval and modern Europe, and finally by the neopagan anti-Semitism of the contemporary era.

It would be an illusion to think that preaching tolerance or even making it an element of education is enough to eradicate ignorance and antipathy. Together, we still have to identify the causes of such fierce tensions.

Choosing to understand and love one another requires acknowledging what still divides us and what cannot be eliminated merely by human determination.

I. Election and Jealousy

It probably was the Jamnia Assembly that, in the year 90, excluded from the synagogue the Jews who had become disciples of Christ. Long before, as early as 50 or 60 AD, Saul of Tarsus — Paul — had tried to arouse the "jealousy" of his Pharisee brothers against the pagans who were followers of the Messiah. As he wrote to the Romans (11:14), he hoped to "make [his] own people jealous, and thus save some of them."

Coming from the pen of Saint Paul, this refers not to arrogant and homicidal envy, but to faithful emulation of divine election. The "jealousy" that Paul expected was not the murderous hatred that seizes Jacob's sons in front of their brother Joseph (Gen 37), but the divine jealousy that is the burning face of God's love.

For Paul the Apostle, this is the key to history, to the election, to the covenant, and to salvation: the "setting aside of the elect" as a "remnant" for "the reconciliation of the world." In this "setting aside," the Scriptures, and especially the prophets Isaiah (11:1; 60:21) and Daniel (11:7) see God cutting a shoot (*necer*) from the holy root, so as to reconcile the world and lead it from death to life (see Rom 11:15).

The double significance of the term "jealousy" in the Bible, where it describes either human self-conceit or the divine care for humanity, induces a double reading of the Scriptures and a double behavior in history.

Among human beings jealousy is a caricature of love, which it aims to imprison and finally chases away. God's jealousy reveals the absolutism of love, the preference of the election, the intransigence of fidelity even when it is abandoned. Human jealousy leads to destroying the object of love; God's jealousy reaches beyond punishment and finally restores life—forever.

What has happened between Jews and Christians over the last twenty centuries is a tragedy of human jealousy usurping divine jealousy. This jealous zeal, which was only too human, took up a different disguise depending on whether those displaying it were Jewish or Christian.

1.

Christian jealousy of Israel very quickly took the shape of a claim for a legacy: just get rid of the other, who is so close and yet so different! The substitution of Jacob for Esau—of the younger son for the elder—has been used as a justification. But then what about Joseph, whom his brothers pretend to murder? This was banishing the youngest so as to retain the privilege of the father's love. So who is who among those biblical figures?

Several of Jesus' parables deal with this issue of the legacy and its appropriation. One of these stories is especially grim. It is the case of the murder of the beloved son, both the eldest and the only one, since the first-born is by definition unique. The parable (Mark 12:1–12) relates the slaying of this son by those who are only asked to take care of the vineyard. The point is that they want to seize it. To anyone who hears this story today, its significance is amazingly ambivalent, as it can be interpreted as foretelling either the killing of Jesus or the killing of Israel, the beloved Son.

The pagans who had become Christians gained access to the Holy Scriptures and to the Jewish festivals. But human—only too human—envy prompted them to marginalize or throw out the Jews. In their first efforts of evangelization, the Apostles Peter and Paul had meant to share with the pagans the grace received by the Jewish people. By celebrating the fulfillment of the messianic promises, the first apostles had generously allowed the pagans to keep a distinct status (Acts 15:5–35) alongside the Jews. But the number and might of the pagans who had entered the church of the Messiah upset and inverted the order of the dispensation of salvation. This movement tended to deprive the Jewish existence of its concrete, carnal, historical contents, and to regard the life of the church, in the present of history, as the final achievement of Jewish hope and life. This was how the theory of substitution was developed.

When speaking of Jews and non-Jews, Paul had stated: "There is no longer Jew or Greek, there is no longer slave or free, there is no longer male and female" (Gal 3:28; see also 1 Cor 12:13). He did not ignore the burdensome time of history and expectation. But in this dazzling insight he announced the achievement of God's plan and the participation of all peoples in the glory of the resurrection.

"The Jews" and "the Nations": these are biblical categories. Where are the Christians then? The ancient way of speaking distinguished between Christian Jews and Christian goyim. We can still find a trace of this on the old Roman mosaic of Saint Sabine (422–430 AD): two figures can be seen on either side of the dedication—they are aging, veiled women holding a book with this caption: *Ecclesia ex circumcisione—Ecclesia ex gentibus.*

The *Ecclesia ex circumcisione* survived as it could. But when Constantine granted the Christians a tolerance that was tantamount to a recognition of Christianity in the life of the state and that eventually resulted in it becoming the religion of the empire, the Jews were brutally rejected. This was a simplistic and unrefined way of denying redemption the time and childbirth labor that it requires, to be completed "that day and hour no one knows," as Jesus says

(Matt 24:36). The mythology of the substitution of the Christian people for the Jewish people fostered a secret, inextinguishable envy and legitimated the taking over of Israel's legacy, of which countless examples could be offered.[4]

This rivalry between brothers gave a specific turn to the relationships between Jews and Christians during the Middle Ages and even in modern times.[5] The best minds knew that the Scriptures were received from the Jews, and also revelation, and—even more fundamentally—the source of salvation. In antiquity, many Christian theologians and spiritual figures learned Hebrew so as to read the Bible in its original language and learn from the rabbis the teachings of their most ancient tradition.

But at the same time, envy introduced an ugly bias in the encounters with Jews, who did not accept Jesus as the Messiah any more than they agreed with the disintegration of their traditions and faithfulness in Christian society, which they considered pagan. This envy prompted many Christians to become involved in passionate polemics. These eventually nurtured anti-Judaism and all of its bloody, tragic manifestations, including the foul calumnies of ritual murder and so many other horrible lies that have reached into our own century through anti-Semitic writings such as the "Protocols of the Elders of Zion."

2.

Can it be said that many Jews[6] reciprocated and replied with corresponding hostility? Those Christians were only goyim! Their claims were ungrounded! All that concerned them and touched them fell into the category of impurity. The only sensible behavior at the time and in the context of exile was to ignore them, to consign them to the same spiritual vacuum as the other pagans. Why, the Jews thought, should Christianity—more than any other non-Jewish religion—be entitled to some special consideration?

Moreover, all those things that specifically represented the Christian faith could only be understood as symbols of the violence and death whose victims were the Jews. These emblems could no longer in any way signify mercy, or forgiveness, or love. They were but horrible pictures, which it was better not to look at, which must not be thought of or mentioned, as forebodings of death and supreme blasphemies!

However, this parallelism of Christian and Jewish spiritual attitudes cannot be further developed, because the balance of power was blatantly unequal. Yet the reciprocity in lack of understanding and contempt remains. Also significant are the affinities and differences that can de detected between Jews' and Christians' respective perceptions of world history.

II. Historical Time and World History

This is another aspect of the twenty-century-old presence of Jewish communities among the Christian nations. The symmetry between the Jewish and Christian destinies proves to be even more contradictory than their attitudes towards the election.

1.

After the last destruction of the temple and the great dispersion, only the synagogue was left to the Jews, if we put aside the Jewish-Christian communities that disappeared little by little.

The Diaspora was then organized under a form of worship in which the priests and the Levites were unable to perform their services, because the ritual sacrifices could no longer be offered. The Jews underwent this new trial, as they had already done during their deportation to Babylon, with a tremendous act of patient and imploring faith, so that God would manifest his glory and fulfill his promises. The whole existence of the Jewish communities was entirely absorbed, in prayer and fidelity, by the accomplishment of their divine vocation. If a Christian notion may be borrowed here, it could be said that this life became "monastic," as had perhaps already been the case with the communities of the Essenes.

For centuries the Jews participated only marginally in human history, limiting themselves to existing and surviving. In some way, they allowed themselves to be buried in history in order to be the witnesses of their faith and of the prophecies. They were hidden inside history and absent from history—except through misfortunes and persecutions. Without a land of their own, having no citizenship, they used the languages of the nations that accepted their particularity, but they kept at the heart of prayer the language of revelation. They were present everywhere and absent from everything.

As it had been deprived of the concrete, historic foundations of its existence by the destruction of the temple and the dispersion of its people across the empires, Israel concentrated all its strength on the expectation of the achievement of history. Until the Age of Enlightenment, Jewish existence deliberately emphasized compliance with the commandments and the study of the law. This separate life aimed at creating the conditions to hasten the glorious final coming of the Messiah. This Jewish existence was entirely centered on the path to the end of history.

2.

The Christians of the nations, as far as they were concerned, should have remained aware that they were offered gratuitously—as a grace that they had not deserved—participation in what God had granted to Israel. But they were permanently tempted, in the course of these last two millennia, to reduce the final accomplishment of the divine plan to the specifics of their own history, whereas the divine plan is something that must continue to be anticipated.

Jesus described to his disciples the time of history as a wake in the night, as the burdensome toil of the servant waiting for his master's return. Christians have too often failed to hear the watchword "patient endurance," as Luke the Evangelist renders it (21:19; 8:15; see Rom 2:7; 5:3; 8:25). It is this patience, through which "you will gain your souls," which allows us to hope in faith, and against all odds, for "the Day of the Lord."

The Christian kingdoms were ambitious to become the historical, temporal realization of the kingdom of heaven. The Church herself often occupied the place of the secular power, presenting herself as the earthly actualization of the kingdom of on high. It was as if the hope for the day to come was absorbed into history, with its incompleteness, and reduced to the temporal present. Such religiosity, which was bound to be oppressive and intolerant, was incomprehensible and, in any case, unacceptable to the Jews whose only king was God and who knew that no kingdom could claim to be God's kingdom, unless it was governed by God himself in peace and justice. Please note in passing that this temporal religiousness was found just as unbearable by the great spiritual figures whom the Holy Spirit has never tired of giving to the Church.

Within the Christian tradition, and repeatedly along the centuries, revival movements like monasticism have provided numerous men and women with a life of sanctity and perfection through obedience to the commandments and the divine precepts. Although the diversity of the times and cultures meant that methods were different, this path towards perfection was comparable to that of the Jewish tradition. Indeed, consecrated life under its multiple forms aims at living within the course of time in a way that is entirely shaped by the messianic expectation. Yet, the existence of this spiritual orientation was no more understandable to most Jews, especially when it took up the appearance of the Spanish Inquisition during the *Reconquista*.

The figure of the suffering innocent, especially as it is described in chapter 53 of Isaiah, remains the point that Jews and Christians keep in common. But this is also where the contradiction reaches its greatest intensity.

First of all, because the faith of any believer, whether he is Jewish or Christian, stumbles over God's incomprehensible injustice. The New Testament describes this trial of faith by the Greek word, *skandalon*. How can its redemptive value be grasped?

In the second place, the very wording of the Scripture suggests that this is a figure of Israel, but also of a messianic character.

The blinding pains of history have obscured the vision of both Christians and Jews, so that we fail to recognize Israel in its Messiah or the Messiah hidden in Israel. Has the time of history been the time of the nations only to allow the seed of Israel to sprout in them?

Jews and Christians have failed to understand each other and scorned each other in the darkness of history. They have also smothered their own hopes for the final gathering. As they are divided in their understanding of the same election and the same expectation, they also have separate outlooks on the promised unity of humankind.

Professor Ady Steg, who is the president of the Universal Israelite Alliance, has recently initiated a biblical study of Isaiah 53,[7] in which Jews and Christians are invited to participate. To my eyes, this common work, done in mutual respect, is an irrefutable sign of the beginning of a new era.

III. The Universality of the Blessing

Universality is the third aspect of the always contradictory symmetry drawn by history between Jews and Christians.

The prophets have clearly announced that one day God will gather all the nations in the knowledge of his name. As Isaiah has the Lord say (66:21), "And I will also take some of them as priests and as Levites." This is the most unthinkable, yet most fundamental, conviction.

1.

During the course of these last two thousand years of history, the Jews were disseminated across the west European and Muslim worlds, as well as in every area where there were Christians in Asia, in Africa, and finally in the New World, in the wake of the great discoveries. During these feverish developments, the Jews who did not strive to gather the nations by associating them with the prayer of the sacerdotal people remained scattered in their exile.

In the nineteenth century, the Jews were charged with being stateless. They were perceived as being a strange network that reached across national boundaries, with a special, mysterious, and threatening solidarity, even though they were actually the guardians of a promised universality, of the unification of all men in one single destiny. According to the very words of God, all men have one single origin and one single vocation. The one God is the God of the whole universe. As a result, all human beings have to consider themselves brothers and sisters, as Adam's children, made in the image and likeness of the God who is their Creator and Father.

The diasporic condition of Israel could have been for humankind the pregnant symbol of this common destiny and of the promised unity. However, either because they deliberately chose to protect themselves or because they were forced to maintain their distinctiveness in order to survive, the Jews lived in their Diaspora by stressing their particularity and preserving their identity behind the fence of the law.

2.

At the same time Christians, who had been pagans of all languages, cultures, and races, were being brought together by their faith in Jesus as Messiah, Son of Israel, and they reacted in a similar way. Christians who receive the entirety of the Holy Scriptures as the Word of God are a living testimony that universalization is being accomplished. And yet Christians have countless times duplicated the historical pattern that had instituted Israel as a nation, preserving their particular languages, ethnic groups, cultures, kingdoms, and empires.

The new *ecclesia* (*qahal*) shrank into historical specificities in many places, even when this meant ignoring its universal vocation and mission. This was the case with the various national churches, of which history gives so many examples, among the peoples of the Middle East, in Byzantium, in the Slavic world, and across the Latin West. That is why for a long time the question in these countries was whether the king or the patriarch, the emperor or the pope, was the head of the Church. National and ethnic divisions remain today the most serious threat to the unity and universal communion that Christians are called to bear witness to and to foster.

But we have entered a new age in the history of humankind, and the fundamental conditions are being turned upside down.

3.

As far as the Jews are concerned, I would like to insist on two points.

First, with the progressive assertion of civil liberties in various European countries since the eighteenth century, many have given up the nearly monastic existence of the Jewish communities and taken part in the great changes of civilization. Along with Christians they have worked for the secular universalism that has based itself on reason and on the ambition of human rights. Jews have often joined Christians in the miscalculations and faults that were caused by human presumption, and when these advances were abrogated, Jews became the primary victims of an unprecedented selective cruelty.

Second, following the example of the European nations and thanks to their participation in the dramatic evolution of civilization and culture, the Jews have managed to create the State of Israel by picking up the standards of a particular national identity.

They have thus radically renewed the question of the Jewish identity, which is now torn between two poles: on the one hand the pole of consecrated life whose only true home is given by God at the end of times; and on the other hand the pole of the secular existence of a people asserting its identity, its language (at long last reconstituted), its ambitions, and its national strength. With Israel the Jewish people has reintegrated the common history of the nations, as a new reference and as a mystery.

4.

Simultaneously, the Catholic Church—and perhaps Christianity as a whole—has begun a journey in the opposite direction. During the contemporary era, the Catholic Church has freed herself, more than ever before, from the domination of princes and from any national identification. While she openly values the latter as cultural wealth, she is opposed to national identification becoming an absolute reference. Her own actions clearly bear witness to this resistance.

At the heart of this movement—and this has been taught explicitly by Christian theologians—lies the rediscovery of faith as a hope immersed in history, and also the rediscovery of the vocation to which are called all those who hear God's Word in what

Jesus said: "Be perfect, therefore, as your heavenly Father is perfect" (Matt 5:48), and, quoting Leviticus (19:2): "You must be holy because I, the Lord your God, am holy."

After the Shoah—but not only because of the Shoah—the determination to recognize and respect the gifts granted to the Jewish people in the history of salvation, and the rediscovery of the perpetuity of the existence of the people of Israel and of its fidelity, are for the Christians the fruit of their rediscovery of their own wealth and vocation. This is not simply a more humane attitude beyond prejudice and hatred.

But ever more unassuming hope is inherent to the messianic faith in God as the Savior. Anticipation of the kingdom of justice and peace leaves Christians with the humbling certainty that they know neither the time nor the hour of the end of history.

The spiritual logic of the blessing recalls the grace of the origin and the loving care of "the promise he made to our ancestors, to Abraham, and to his descendants forever" (Luke 1:55), and to "all the families of the earth" (Gen 12:3).

This is the task which the Catholic Church and many Christians want to carry out today. Of course, one confession must be added immediately. This new awareness was encapsulated for the Catholic Church in the Second Vatican Council's *Nostra Aetate* Declaration. In the last thirty years it has given way to many comments, especially on the initiatives of Pope John Paul II. However, this new understanding still has to thoroughly remodel the ideas of many peoples who belong to the Christian sphere but whose heart has not yet been purified by the Spirit of the Messiah. Historical experience shows us that lasting "patience" and many educational efforts are required to appropriate one's soul (cf. Luke 21:19).

Nevertheless, there is no veering from the direction we are now taking. This is part of the movement through which humankind is being united, even at the cost of confrontations. This orientation testifies to the Catholic Church's determination to carry out her mission in the service of this world, to do the will of the Creator of Israel and the Redeemer of humanity.

8
Where Jews and Christians Work Together

Cardinal Lustiger's address to the World Jewish Congress, New York, February 10, 2003. Translated by Jean Duchesne.

Dear friends, you are all aware of the major events in the relationships between Jews and Christians since the end of the Second World War, including (more recently) Pope John Paul II's visit to Rome's Great Synagogue on the 13th of April, 1986, and his prayer at the Western Wall in Jerusalem on the 26th of March, 2000.

The last half-century has been marked by a "renewal of ties" between Jews and Christians. This does not signify an attempt to rewrite history, but a genuine repentance on the part of the Catholic Church for all the wounds and wrongs inflicted in the past.

♦

I find it striking, if not deeply moving, that in so few years, on both the Jewish and the Catholic sides, even the least well informed people should have grasped the significance and the relevance of such events. The past has not been forgotten, the suffering has not been erased, the differences cannot be wiped away, and the sometimes radical disagreements cannot be obliterated. Yet, misgivings and resentment have disappeared, while mutual trust, respect, and friendship at long last allow real dialogue, real explorations, and real discoveries, according to the wealth and gifts received on each side. For the goal is neither to gain the upper hand, even by peaceful means, nor to bargain for some kind of a deal, as is the case in business or politics.

Modernity has liberated the relationships between Jews and Christians from their old, strictly "bilateral" patterns, opening up them both to a "third party" that they have to confront together.

Modernity is an opportunity: because it places us both in similar situations, it allows us to evade the narrowness of one-to-one encounters, and this is what makes possible an actual "renewal of ties." People can love each other better when they are looking in the same direction than when they watch each other.

As a result, an essential part of Jewish-Christian dialogue is to answer the questions that confront both of us.

Confronting our differences will allow each side more clearly to identify its actual position, and that of the other, while respecting each one's uniqueness, as Pope John Paul II suggested on October 28th, 1985.

Which of the challenges of modernity does the Jewish or Christian consciousness feel prepared to take up? Under what forms can the Jewish or Christian collective identity assert itself in the modern world? Or, more synthetically, which goals, among those set up by modernity, can be adopted by Jewish or Christian consciousness? What means to reach these goals are available to that consciousness?

♦

In the first place, we must fight together for *the cause of humanity, of human dignity, and of human rights*.

Human rights were first stated in the American Declaration of Independence of 1776, and this led to the Universal Declaration of Human Rights of 1948, under the authority of René Cassin at the Palais de Chaillot in Paris. Human rights may seem to have been invented by modernity. And yet, those who have received for several millennia the gift of the Torah can find in it the true source and foundation of man's paramount dignity.

As Jews and Christians, we both refer to the first two chapters of Genesis. To the question put forth in Psalm 8 (verse 4)—"What are human beings that you are mindful of them, mortals that you care for them?"—Jews and Christians receive the same answer: "God created man in his image and semblance." The relationship between the one God and man, his creature, is for us the rock upon which we can build the search for a rational foundation of human dignity, of the dignity of any human creature. For, as Rachi Berechit wrote, only man was somehow created by God's hand. This is what is expressed in Psalm 139 (verse 5): "O Lord, you...lay your hand upon me."

In the eighteenth century, under the influence of the Enlightenment, political rights were asserted from a rationalist perspective that was often foreign to religions and certainly hostile to the church. However, the notions of civil rights and religious freedom, as well as that of tolerance, had appeared as early as the sixteenth century. Anyway, one of the first consequences was the emancipation of Jews throughout Europe.

Meanwhile, for all Christians, and especially for Catholics, this was the beginning of a time of antireligious repression and even persecution. Things having thus been turned round, the minorities that used to be oppressed, or whose rights used to be ignored, were triumphing over their former persecutors, and running the risk of becoming persecutors in their turn! Such reversal of roles is not unheard of.

What is remarkable today, nevertheless, is that Jews and Christians agree to promote human rights because they both acknowledge the universal *berit* that the Creator entered into with humankind, according to Exodus 19:5: "The whole earth is mine."

Yet, the universalism of human rights as rooted in the universality of reason is currently being challenged among sizable portions of humanity. This is the case, for example, within the Chinese empire, or among the Islamic nations where the Universal Declaration of Human Rights is considered as a mere by-product of Western culture. Westerners are then requested to accept other approaches to human rights, and to give up what is branded as a remnant of colonial imperialism.

Moreover, the very significance of human rights can vary with public opinion in western democracies. The foundation, then, no longer is the supposedly absolute and universal rationality of the eighteenth century. This is a serious challenge, as the stakes are no less than the unity of humankind and the universality of every person's rights and duties toward all others. And this is where Jews and Christians have to work together, so as to point out the rational foundation that can impose itself to all humans in the name of their condition. How paradoxical it is that proclaiming the universality of human rights should bring us back to the top of Mount Sinai, to revelation, and to the gift of the law!

Yet, this is indisputably our common urgent mission, and it is twofold: first we have to study together the rational foundation of the universality that human rights implies and demands; and second, we have to enter into dialogue and action with the other cultures and religions of Asia, with Muslim countries, etc., so as to serve humanity as a whole through the diversity of its cultures.

◆

Then, after human rights, there are a number of *moral issues*. What we often call "ethical" questions seem to be reemerging forcefully in the management of social and individual lives as well as in the adaptation to the technological and economic advances of humanity. This is obvious in the field of the sciences of life, from genetic engineering to the numerous problems raised by medical progress. And it is no less obvious at the economic and social levels, concerning the respective status of man and woman, or of minorities, etc., in international relations.

I am not sure whether this return of moral issues is as new and surprising in the United States as it seems to be for European public opinion. For us in Europe, and especially in France, such a reappearance of morals or ethics in the social, political, economic, scientific, and technological realms looks somewhat unexpected and disturbing. The point is that our culture has deluded itself into assuming that scientific rationality would automatically guarantee moral improvement.

If we are to take up this challenge, where do we start from as believers?

In the course of its history, mainly during the second millennium, Christianity has progressively developed a reflection fostered by the tradition of the Bible and the Gospel, and aimed at basing action on reason. That was how, from the twelfth or thirteenth century until the modern times, a whole corpus of doctrine took shape, grounded on "natural law." It has evolved together with philosophical reflection on human action. John Rawls' work can be understood in this perspective, even if it can be criticized in the name of the traditional teachings of Catholic morals. In this respect, the famous maxim of the Talmudic masters can be of some help: "No one denies that idolatry is absurd, but people irresistibly resort to it to justify moral licentiousness."

The Catholic Church has endeavored to redefine and actualize the demands of morals in our century, without giving up the wealth of her reflection on human action. To do so, she has deliberately focused on the biblical phrasing of the Ten Words or Commandments, as Exodus (chapter 20) and Deuteronomy (chapter 5) have recorded them for us.

The Christian faith thus strives, as it has done at numerous points during the past centuries, to tap the source of God's Word so that human beings may receive life and act accordingly. As Psalm 119 puts it, "Your righteousness is an everlasting righteousness, and your law is the truth" (verse 142); "Your decrees are righteous forever; give me understanding that I may live" (verse 144).

The Jewish tradition has ceaselessly studied the commandments, all the commandments. It will be enough here simply to mention the names of Maimonides, Abravanel, Crescas, and countless others whose works were developed along parallel lines with those of contemporary Christian authors. Does not today's restored convergence between Jews and Christians call for renewed ambition for human intelligence? The task is to develop the wealth of revelation and of God's commandments in the field of moral and ethical rationality. Thinkers and philosophers like Paul Ricoeur on the Christian side, and Emmanuel Levinas on the Jewish side, but also Leo Strauss and Hannah Arendt, have made possible that indispensable meditative reflection that rediscovers the sources and expands toward the time ahead. It seems remarkable to me that Pope John Paul II should have relied on Ricoeur and Levinas, among others, in his personal thinking, and in order to revive the thinking of the Church.

It goes without saying that such necessary theoretical research should lead, as has already been often the case, to explicit common pronouncements on the concrete choices on which the future of humankind depends.

♦

Now, a third area in which common reflections must be developed is *politics*. Now more than ever, at the dawn of the third millennium, the problems raised by politics are an invitation for Jews and Christians to reach deeper together in their reflections, and to act together. This concerns power, the exercise of power, the organization of social life, and the recognition that democracy is, among the various forms of government currently existing in the world, the one that respects "least badly" the rights of each person.

Political issues and questions about the use of power can be found at the heart of all civilizations. Biblical revelation is capable of providing our global civilization with the consistency and the stability it needs. I will limit myself to two aspects.

First, biblical revelation offers a historical vision of human destiny, from creation to final judgment. Man can thus locate himself and the whole universe in a relationship with his Creator and Redeemer.

And this leads to the second aspect, which is the tireless criticism of man's power over man. In biblical history, the only one whose authority not only respects human liberty but actually founds it is God himself. The first verse of Psalm 72 reads, "Give the king your judgments, O God, and your justice to this king's son."

The Torah and the prophets point out the weaknesses of human power when confronted with the revelation of the one God, while the other writings teach the wisdom that is required if human beings are to welcome the destiny in which the divine mercy and justice are revealed.

This is our common biblical background, which the New Testament has certainly not denied, but rather reasserted! It is now offered to global consciousness as a treasure for humanity.

However, both on the Jewish and on the Christian sides, human reason has ceaselessly been tempted to cheapen this treasure. Numerous Jewish and Christian thinkers have striven to take up this challenge along criss-crossing lines, and their works enlighten one another. I wish to point out here the importance for Jewish thought of the criticism of Hegel's political theories by Franz Rosenzweig. This is a reflection that should prove decisive in the future. If we want to realize how crucial these theoretical questions are, we only need recall the episodes of the Nazi or Communist totalitarianisms in the twentieth century.

It is obvious that the management of world affairs never stops posing formidable questions to the human consciousness. The pope's own appeals keep global public opinion on the alert. Thoughtful exchanges between Jews and Christians, rooted in their common background and disdaining polemics and emotions, are more necessary than ever to help humankind find the ways to peace and harmony for the good of all.

♦

A fourth domain where Jewish and Christian religious ideas have to operate in cooperation is in the area of *modern rational criticism*.

How have we responded to this so far? We must acknowledge that our reactions have not been absolutely similar in time, manner, and content. Both the Christian and the Jewish faiths have had to face the criticisms of rationalism, be it simply deist or downright atheistic. The names of Voltaire and Diderot might suffice here to characterize such defiance. The most radical challenge, however, came from German thought. It was often Protestant in its origin, and might be said to have been represented most significantly by Hegel's philosophy, as all his efforts amounted to a historical criticism of the Bible.

Such criticism did grant the biblical narratives a moral or

poetic value. Yet it denied any credibility to what they asserted, and faith in the Word of revelation thus seemed to become impossible. All the biblical texts, including the New Testament, were submitted to such dissection. Still, we should note that the Jewish and Christian exegetical traditions had not missed the issues raised by criticism: these had already been tackled very early by Abraham Ibn Ezra as well as by Jerome and Origen in ancient times.

On the Jewish side, the Haskalah did integrate this research. However, the whole structure of Jewish piety, and therefore of Jewish practice, was deeply upset by the logic of assimilation and integration into Christian societies, which were themselves drifting away from their religious practices and traditions.

On the Christian side, what was called "fideism" and "pietism" consisted in the same individual thinking alternately, if not simultaneously, at two different, totally disconnected, levels—that of critical rationality, and that of emotional fervor.

Assimilation and secularization thus appear as internal problems, inherent in the common condition of Jews and Christians as believers. On their respective sides, they have both had to rediscover and "reinvent from scratch," as it were, their relationships to their traditions.

But today we have already entered an era when thought has gone beyond assimilation, which has itself outlived the period of secularization. This was at least how Levinas would characterize our situation.

Patient efforts have been made, fed by wonderful creativity and fervor, to restore among the ruins the legitimacy of faith under the scrutiny of reason. Epistemological research has led to the criticism of criticism, and borne new intellectual and spiritual fruit in the interpretation and understanding of the Scriptures.

Eminent Jewish and Christian thinkers—exegetes, philosophers, theologians—have achieved major results, which have brought about, among other advances, renewed mutual interest between Jews and Christians. We can give as examples Buber's thesis on Nicholas of Cues, Rosenzweig's appropriation of Kierkegaard's criticism of Hegel, Scholem's discovery of the Kabbala thanks to the works of the Christian thinker Molitor, Hannah Arendt's work on Augustine, Heschel's book on Kierkegaard and Menahem Mendel of Kotzk, etc.

It would be very useful to write a history of this confrontation with modern criticism, and to study how faith has managed to withstand the challenge of modernity and remains on its course both in Judaism and in Christianity, which are rooted in the same origin: the Bible itself.

♦

A fifth issue for both Jews and Christian today is *religious encounters*. It is a novel, often dramatically pressing, challenge. All around the world, the intermixing of various populations now brings side by side very different religious faiths, and this leads to unprecedented confrontations.

Jews and Christians are the guardians of the revelation of the one God and of his plan to bring all humans together one day. Such election and promise are summarized in the call and blessing addressed to Abraham. The election points to the singular destiny of one people. The universalism of the promise concerns all the nations and the whole history of humankind.

The question then is how to understand the current religious diversity in the light of such a revelation. Some thinkers have opposed Jewish particularism to Christian universalism. According to them, Jewish particularism would leave to non-Jews no more than Noah's covenant, while Christian universalism would be implicitly achieved through the relationship of the human consciousness with God, even if the latter remains unknown or ignored. Such a vision is blatantly unacceptable and must be criticized in the name of tradition itself.

On the Jewish side, the Holy Scripture already testifies unambiguously to a covenant with Adam, since Hosea (6:7) claims that Adam "violated" that covenant. Six of the seven commandments given to Noah were linked by the Sages (*Sanhedrin*, 586)[1] to the ones given to Adam in Genesis, 2:17. Let us also note the recurring scriptural motif of the nations "forgetting the one God." The very call for them virtually to become converts by "remembering the covenant with Noah" implies that they have forgotten and violated that covenant. Conversion then is some kind of a restoration of the original order. If indeed this is the case, the tradition of Israel is the first that transcends strictly ethnic standards (since one can *become* a Jew), and we can find here the first unraveling between religion and a national identity. This was later confirmed by the introduction of successive stages in conversion, for example with the "God-fearing" class in ancient times.

The pagan world, then, proves not to be all of one piece. Areas of varying closeness can be identified. Christian universalism then appears to be not a denial, but a continuation of this vision. A figure like that of Ruth—the classical reference in most reflections on the goyim—can become a source of inspiration in today's situation: her story places common life before the religious question.

To sum up, these theoretical starting points deserve to be investigated and compared peacefully between Jews and Christians. They ought to foster a common meditation on the hope given by the promise made to Abraham: through you "shall all the nations of the earth gain blessing" (Gen 22:18).

However, we cannot wait to ask, How and on what bases can respectful dialogue with the other religions be launched for the good of all humankind?

In Europe and in North America, this has already become an almost commonplace experience. But the limits of such encounters have also been quickly experienced, perhaps because Jews as well as Christians have not thought hard enough together about the theoretical foundations of such dialogue.

In this respect, Pope John Paul II has taken a series of bold initiatives: the interreligious meetings of Assisi in 1986, 1993, 1999. He invited representatives of all the religions in the world to get together, with their differences and specificities, and without any confusion at the level of their beliefs or forms of prayer. And he asked them all to work together for peace, inasmuch as each of them testifies to man's search for God. These meetings have been most significant, but they also call for urgent theoretical explorations and practical reflections.

♦

I now have a sixth and final point to raise: in *our pluralist societies*, what concrete shapes can *the group of believers*—Jews on the one side, Christians on the other—take up against the background of globalization?

This is a particularly sensitive issue. It does not depend only on sociological observations, but also on the free choices made by believers. And the social consequences are crucial, for the members of the community, whether Jewish or Christian, as well as for the other members of the society where they belong.

Jews and Christians each used to live as homogeneous groups, and this may still be the case today.

As far as Christians are concerned, when this homogeneity coincided with a whole people, it gave what historians have called "Christendom." From the village to the nation, the whole society was claimed to be "part of" the Church. That homogeneous society asked itself no questions about its existence, but was confronted by the internal conflicts that are inherent in any society based on the distinction between the religious and political powers.

For one and a half millennia, Jews were considered the only "foreign" body in that society, even though Jewish communities had sometimes been settled long before whole nations were converted to Christianity. Those Jewish minorities made up homogeneous groups, simply to remain able to lead a life characterized by consciously different behavior, religious practices, and traditions. In fact, those minorities also made up homogeneous societies. I will not evoke here all the frictions, rejections, and persecutions that this entailed in the course of history.

My question will rather be whether such homogeneity still exists on the Christian side these days. You all know that there are persecuted Christian minorities today.

Anyway, Christian homogeneity certainly is a much less massive phenomenon, and its consistency varies with the free choices made by the members of the churches. Some institutional remnants can be detected here and there, for example in England, where the national church is still linked to the sovereign. Does today's Russia play in the same league, given the virtually official relationship between the Russian government and the church there? Also, what about Greece? And as far as Judaism is concerned, let me ask as well, What about the State of Israel?

I will not deal with the case of other religions, especially Islam and all the nations that claim to make up Muslim states. I will also refrain from addressing the case of those Asian countries where a religious majority dominates the organization of social and political life.

What we have to face first is the fact that Europe and the New World have become pluralist societies whose political structures are generally liberal and democratic.

In such a context, what is the most coherent strategy for the practice of Jewish life and Christian faithfulness? How can deliberate or instinctive choices identify our religious groups in these pluralist societies?

This question has been of paramount importance in all Western Christian countries over the last two centuries. Christian organizations of all kinds have been born, both Catholic and Protestant: trade unions, hospitals, schools, clubs, newspapers and media groups, even political parties.

In this respect, and especially in France, and perhaps more there than anywhere else in Western Europe, we have had a specific experience, which can be summed up in two words that may be somewhat difficult to understand from outside.

First, there is what we called "*la laïcité*," and this can hardly be rendered by the fact of "secularization," or (even less) by the ideology of "secularism," as it goes much further than the separation of church and state and rather expresses the point of view of the civil society.

Then there is, from the Church's point of view, the "Christian presence in the world." This has been a retrieval in the last few decades of a notion that had been familiar to the early generations of Christian groups within the much larger Roman Empire, as described in the *Epistle to Diognetus*.

On the contrary, the French are often surprised to find in the United States a free and pluralist society where each group asserts itself quite distinctly, even in housing, with identifiable neighborhoods, which actually does not in the least undermine the democratic ideal.

At this level, the options are diametrically opposed. Here in New York, I visited last year a number of important Jewish communities that were homogeneous in their spiritual and practical choices. Their fervor and strict observance obviously did not prevent the members of those communities from taking part actively in contemporary culture and modern life, insofar as they considered this compatible with their religious commitment.

Those Jews have managed to offer an answer to the fundamental question that both Christian and Jewish communities have to face worldwide. And this question is, How do we reconcile the history and geography of our communities with the history and geography of modernity? Perhaps nowhere else than here in New York has a better answer been experienced.

Of course, Jews and Christians have quite different ways of considering religious practices and obligations. Yet it would certainly be highly stimulating and most fruitful to compare the ecclesial lifestyle with that of Jewish communities. This would require great mutual respect, and overcoming all kinds of prejudices. But a better understanding of the relationship between faith and human existence in its daily, practical realities would become possible.

Such investigations would quickly lead to such key biblical notions as "the people of God" ("my people," as the Lord says, or "the assembly of God," the *qahal*) where the word *ecclesia* (church) comes from. These two notions are not contradictory. They deserve a theoretical reflection, while their historical relationship should be investigated as well.

◆

So these were six points, among many others, that we should study together, Jews and Christians. By discovering another self, different and yet so close, everyone might come to understand himself better, and all might then become able to ask more forcefully the questions that are vital today for the future of humankind.

Because of God's Word, and because of all that we share in faith, our duty is to work for the good of all people, in obedience to the will of our unique Creator and Father.

Thank you for your attention.

Afterword
Rabbi Alan Brill, PhD

(Cooperman/Ross Endowed Professor, in honor of Sister Rose Thering, in the graduate department of Jewish-Christian studies, Seton Hall University.)

"What a long way we have come together, we Jews and Catholics, in more than half a century!" With these words, Cardinal Jean-Marie Lustiger reflected on how the Second Vatican Council was a hermeneutic revision, a fundamental change in Jewish-Christian relations. He proclaimed that not since Paul and the council of Jerusalem two millennia ago had the church acknowledged so plainly the common roots and continuous vocation of the Jewish people from which she is issued. Yet Cardinal Lustiger emphasized that the task to remodel Christian understanding of Jews and Judaism was not complete. As part of this of process of understanding, I am honored to write an afterword to this volume of speeches and interviews of Cardinal Jean-Marie Lustiger—a man who sought rapprochement between the Jewish and Christian faiths after two millennia of alienation.

In his addresses, Cardinal Lustiger made it clear that he saw the Gospel as a direct continuity of Judaism. To establish this continuity, Cardinal Lustiger set forth his theology of Judaism from a Catholic perspective. Jews are the chosen people, the ones who bring Abraham's promise of universal salvation to the world. For Lustiger, this was a key idea in both Judaism and Christianity. The hermeneutic revision of Vatican II requires that Judaism should not be portrayed as rejected, carnal, or cursed. Rather, Judaism, its mission, its message, and its faith are fundamentally the same as Christianity. Lustiger sees Christianity as an "open Judaism."

For Lustiger, the Jewish covenant is fulfilled in Christianity, which transcends Judaism by bringing the covenant to all humanity. He offered a novel spin on the traditional doctrine of the witness. Israel must remain faithful to Judaism because of their covenant, which is not just in the past but ongoing in history and revelation. He added that a genuine understanding of the divine plan for the *eschaton* cannot include the idea that Judaism will be "replaced."

Yet, as a Jew, I do not identify with this reading of Judaism through the Apostle Paul's vision of an Abrahamic promise. I do not hear in it the living faith of Judaism as expressed in Jewish theology.

A foundational concept of Jewish theology is that God took the Jews out of Egypt to be his special nation. In accordance with their special status with God, the Jews were given the commandments at Sinai and the land of Israel as a possession.

Jews do not need to open up God's covenant to bring it to the world since, according to Judaism, all righteous people have a natural access to God, without a need for a specific covenant. How do Jews define covenant? The covenant is the special bond of Torah, Sabbath, and circumcision. Judaism has separate universal and covenantal aspects. As Rabbi Joseph Soloveitchik wrote: "Even as the Jew is moved by his private Sinaitic Covenant with God to embody and preserve the teachings of the Torah, he is committed to the belief that all mankind…is 'in His image' and is possessed of an inherent human dignity and worthiness." Cardinal Lustiger, however, specifically criticized the rabbinic Noahide laws as not universalist enough, thus requiring Christianity to add a greater universal dimension to Judaism.

A second theme in these talks is Lustiger's attempt to come to grips with anti-Semitism. "Christians have opened their eyes to Jewish pain," requiring an examination of conscience for their role in fostering a culture of anti-Semitism. His noble conclusion after the examination was that there could not be Christian anti-Semitism. Any reading of Christianity that taught that there was a need for the persecution and punishment of Israel was a misreading of Christianity. But for many, questions will remain. Didn't anti-Semitic rhetoric start in the patristic period? Are not the church's teachings on Judaism ones of contempt and degradation? And was not the church responsible for ritual murder, segregation, the badge, and the myth of the wandering Jew? Lustiger replied: "History and sociology may support your opinion, but it is not true from the point of view of faith and theology." That is, Judaism and Christianity are theologically connected and cannot have enmity between them. Nevertheless, Lustiger acknowledged that the Europeans, as inheritors of Christian culture, bear responsibility for their historical actions.

How can Christianity come to terms with the animosity of the past? One of Lustiger's assertions was that Christians continue to maintain a pagan mentality. For Lustiger, Christianity that is not grounded in Judaism reverts back to mythology, violence, and idolatry of the self. For Lustiger, the Shoah was the mystery of lawlessness (2 Thess 2:7), evidence that the nations needed repentance and a return to the church.

He also asserted that the immense *tremendum* of the Holocaust fulfilled the typology of the suffering servant of Isaiah 53, the suffering of the messiah. The people of Israel were the bearers of revelation about humanity's need for goodness and dignity. But from a Jewish point of view, if the theological understanding for the murder of six million Jews is messianic suffering, the unique elements of the extermination camps with their horrific forms of degradation are forgotten beside the light of faith.

Finally, it is important to remember that Jean-Marie Lustiger was born Jewish, as "Aron Lustiger." He wrote, "I've always considered myself a Jew, even if that's not the opinion of some rabbis," who insist that "a Jew becoming a Christian does not take up authentic Judaism, but turns his back to it."

Several years ago, Cardinal Lustiger lead a group of cardinals and bishops in visiting a wide range of Jewish institutions in New York, in order to see Judaism as a living religion. Among the rabbis they visited was the Hasidic Bobover rebbe, who blessed Cardinal Lustiger and the visiting group in their continuing work as righteous Gentiles. We look forward to the day when the blessing of good work will fully blossom and when Cardinal Lustiger's fellow Christians will go forth to complete Vatican II's hermeneutic revision by living out more fully and authentically their deeper understanding of the Jewish faith and people.

Notes

(Cardinal Lustiger's notes are so indicated. All other notes are editorial or translator's notes).

CHAPTER ONE

1. This tendency existed among the first settlers of Israel and recommended the abandonment of their Jewish character. Later the movement urged the Jews in Israel to merge with non-Jews and to create a local political and cultural system.

2. But the people refused to listen to the voice of Samuel; they said, 'No! but we are determined to have a king over us, so that we also may be like other nations....'" (1 Sam. 8:19).

3. *Alyah*, literally a "going up": the return of the Jews to the land of Israel.

4. *Sabra* is the Barbary fig, which is hard on the outside but sweet inside. It is the nickname for Jews born in Israel.

5. Berck is a resort on the North Sea. It was famous for its invigorating air, and many sick people, especially children, went there in hope of cures.

6. The covenant with the sons of Noah (Gen 9:8–10) is considered in the rabbinic tradition as a covenant that is continually on offer to the nations.

7. Goyim, the plural of goy, the "nations," used of non-Jewish peoples.

8. *Qahal*, "assembly," "convocation," "congregation."

9. "No doubt some of the branches have been cut off, and, like shoots of wild olive, you have been grafted among the rest to share with them the rich sap provided by the olive tree itself, but still, even if you think yourself superior to the other branches, remember that you do not support the root; it is the root that supports you" (Rom 11:17–18).

10. Drancy was a transit camp, harshly administered by French police, where Jews awaited transportation to Auschwitz.

11. Since the Middle Ages, the Jews of Spain were called Sephardic, and the name was extended to the Jews of the Mediterranean areas generally. Ashkenazi applies, since the same period, to the Jews of Germany and central and northern Europe.

12. Shoah. Hebrew for "annihilation."

13. Hanukkah was instituted in 165 BC by Judas Maccabacus to mark the purification of the temple after its profanation by Antiochus Epiphanes. It is the feast of Dedication or of Lights. Jews light candles on eight consecutive days, starting on 25 Kislev.

14. After the ten plagues of Egypt, the Hebrews were allowed to depart and to pass through the Red Sea. Passover (*Pesach*) is the feast of passage that commemorates the Exodus; Jews have their meal that day in traveling clothes. To it has been associated a feast of first fruits that involves the sacrifice of a lamb or a young goat whose blood is put on the doorposts and lintels.

CHAPTER TWO

1. This is the first word, used as a title, of the Hebrew text of Jeremiah's Lamentations. [Cardinal Lustiger's note].

2. According to the normative interpretation of the Midrash.

CHAPTER THREE

1. Arianism, a Christian heresy initiated by Arius of Alexandria, was condemned at the Council of Nicaea in 325.

2. Henri de Lubac (1896–1991) was a French Jesuit theologian and historian who was made a cardinal by John Paul II in 1983. The work referred to is *L'Exégèse médiévale*.

3. Charles Maurras (1869–1952), a French writer and political activist of the extreme right, was a cofounder of *l'Action française* and attacked what he thought to be the causes of disorder in art and political life.

4. Jules Isaac (1877–1963) was one of the prominent secularized French Jewish thinkers at the turn of the century and an author of the Third Republic's "official" history.

5. Théodore Reinach (1860–1928) was a French Jew who became a lawyer, then a university professor, and finally a politician. He worked for the assimilation of Jews into French society and culture. Marcel Simon (1907–1986) was a historian of religions and a specialist of Christian-Jewish relations during the era of the early church.

6. The red and white "little wheel" that Jews were forced to wear as a mark of identification in fourteenth-century France.

7. Spanish Jews who were forced to convert in the fifteenth century, among whom certain ones remained secretly faithful to the Jewish religion.

8. The Parousia is the second coming of Christ in glory.

9. Falashas are Ethiopian Jews who lived for centuries isolated from the rest of the Jewish community. Some of them recently immigrated to Israel.

CHAPTER FIVE

1. *Kol Nidrei* is a prayer recited in the synagogue before the beginning of the evening service on Yom Kippur, the Day of Atonement. Kaddish is an important prayer in the Jewish liturgy.

2. The *Epistle to Diognetus* is an early work of Christian Apologetics usually dated to the late second century.

CHAPTER SIX

1. Saul Friedländer, *Reflections of Nazism—An Essay on Kitsch and Death*, trans. Thomas Weyr (New York: Harper & Row, 1982), 136.
2. Ibid., 123.
3. Ibid., 102–4.
4. Ibid., 89.
5. Ibid., 105.
6. Ibid., 103.

CHAPTER SEVEN

1. You have in your hands the Declaration *Nostra Aetate* that was solemnly adopted by the Second Vatican Council on October 28, 1965. You also have the French bishops' Declaration that was released on September 30, 1997, at the Memorial of Drancy, the place of deportation of practically all of the 75,000 Jewish victims who were French residents who were sent to the extermination camps. You are also familiar with the Holy See's Declaration in its English original as it was published at the Vatican on March 12, 1998, under the title: "We remember. Reflections on the Shoah." Finally, I wish to mention Cardinal Edward Idris Cassidy's address to the American Jewish Committee in Washington, DC on May 15, 1998. These four documents complement each other, and they recall a number of facts and circumstances that I will not repeat here. [Cardinal Lustiger's note].

2. The authorized ecclesial Declarations mentioned in note one accomplish a return on the past. They put an end to the teaching of contempt. They turn our minds towards the future, as John Paul II wished in his letter to Cardinal Cassidy approving the Roman document on the Shoah: "May memory play its necessary role in the process of the building up of a future where the unspeakable iniquity of the Shoah will become forever impossible. May the Lord of history guide the efforts of Catholics and Jews, as well as of all men and women of good will, so that they may work together

for a world where the life and dignity of each human being will be genuinely respected, since all have been created in God's image and resemblance."

3. The demarcation line divided France into two zones: one occupied by the Germans, and one under the control of the Vichy government [Cardinal Lustiger's note].

4. I will mention only one: the French kings claim to descend from David. This led their advisors to have them crowned according to the ritual designed for the kings of Israel, as described in the Bible. This had already been done in Byzantium. See for instance Marquis de la Franquerie, *Ascendances davidiques des rois de France…*(*de France* éditions Sainte Jeanne d'Arc, 1984, 79) [Cardinal Lustiger's note].

5. One cannot honestly ignore the fourth century and the beginning of anti-Jewish rationalization, particularly with St. Cyrillus of Jerusalem. The theory of substitution was elaborated by the church fathers [Cardinal Lustiger's note].

6. Many Jews, but not all of them: before the Christians started rethinking the role of Judaism positively, the Jews had acknowledged with Maimonides that Christianity had been given a certain mission [Cardinal Lustiger's note].

7. This is how Professor Steg explained the goal of this work, under the authority of the College of Jewish Studies:

> Chapter 53 of the prophet Isaiah has undoubtedly been one of the most controversial texts in the history of monotheism. In the foretelling of the messianic drama, Christians saw a prefiguration of Christ's Passion, while Jews read the story of the trials of Israel in its exile. However, beyond the eschatological stakes, the idea of redemption through suffering does sound even more forceful in Isaiah's words.
>
> Does suffering play a role in the history of **gueula** (redemption)? Might not this interpretation distort Isaiah's words by giving them a significance that they do not have?

At a time when democracies tend to be overcome by victim morals, can the study of these verses help us to clarify the question? What do both Jewish and Christian theologians and psychoanalysts have to say on the place of suffering in the human condition? [Cardinal Lustiger's note].

CHAPTER EIGHT

1. *Sanhedrin* is one of the tractates of the *Nezikin*, the section of the Talmud dealing with civil and criminal proceedings.

Eugene J. Fisher and Leon Klenicki, editors, *In Our Time: The Flowering of Jewish-Catholic Dialogue* (A Stimulus Book, 1990).

David Burrell and Yehezkel Landau, editors, *Voices from Jerusalem* (A Stimulus Book, 1991).

Leon Klenicki, editor, *Toward A Theological Encounter* (A Stimulus Book, 1991).

John Rousmaniere, *A Bridge to Dialogue: The Story of Jewish-Christian Relations,* edited by James A. Carpenter and Leon Klenicki (A Stimulus Book, 1991).

Michael E. Lodahl, *Shekhinah/Spirit* (A Stimulus Book, 1992).

George M. Smiga, *Pain and Polemic: Anti-Judaism in the Gospels* (A Stimulus Book, 1992).

Eugene J. Fisher, editor, *Interwoven Destinies: Jews and Christians Through the Ages* (A Stimulus Book, 1993).

Anthony Kenny, *Catholics, Jews and the State of Israel* (A Stimulus Book, 1993).

Bernard J. Lee, SM, *Jesus and the Metaphors of God: The Christs of the New Testament,* Conversation on the Road Not Taken, Vol. 2 (A Stimulus Book, 1993).

Eugene J. Fisher, editor, *Visions of the Other: Jewish and Christian Theologians Assess the Dialogue* (A Stimulus Book, 1995).

Leon Klenicki and Geoffrey Wigoder, editors, *A Dictionary of the Jewish-Christian Dialogue,* Expanded Edition (A Stimulus Book, 1995).

Vincent Martin, *A House Divided: The Parting of the Ways between Synagogue and Church* (A Stimulus Book, 1995).

Philip A. Cunningham and Arthur F. Starr, editors, *Sharing Shalom: A Process for Local Interfaith Dialogue Between Christians and Jews* (A Stimulus Book, 1998).

Frank E. Eakin, Jr., *What Price Prejudice? Christian Antisemitism in America* (A Stimulus Book, 1998).

Ekkehard Schuster and Reinhold Boschert-Kimmig, *Hope Against Hope: Johann Baptist Metz and Elie Wiesel Speak Out on the Holocaust* (A Stimulus Book, 1999).

Mary C. Boys, *Has God Only One Blessing? Judaism as a Source of Christian Understanding* (A Stimulus Book, 2000).

Avery Dulles, SJ, and Leon Klenicki, editors, *The Holocaust, Never to Be Forgotten: Reflections on the Holy See's Document* We Remember (A Stimulus Book, 2000).

Johannes Reuchlin, *Recommendation Whether to Confiscate, Destroy and Burn All Jewish Books: A Classic Treatise against Anti-Semitism*, translated, edited, and with an introduction by Peter Wortsman (A Stimulus Book, 2000).

Philip A. Cunningham, *A Story of Shalom: The Calling of Christians and Jews by a Covenanting God* (A Stimulus Book, 2001).

Philip A. Cunningham, *Sharing the Scriptures*, The Word Set Free, Vol. 1 (A Stimulus Book, 2003).

Dina Wardi, *Auschwitz: Contemporary Jewish and Christian Encounters* (A Stimulus Book, 2003).

Michael Lotker, *A Christian's Guide to Judaism* (A Stimulus Book, 2004).

Lawrence Boadt and Kevin di Camillo, editors, *John Paul II in the Holy Land: In His Own Words: With Christian and Jewish Perspectives by Yehezkel Landau and Michael McGarry, CSP* (A Stimulus Book, 2005).

James K. Aitken and Edward Kessler, editors, *Challenges in Jewish-Christian Relations* (A Stimulus Book, 2006).

George M. Smiga, *Gospel of John Set Free, The: Preaching without Anti-Judaism* (A Stimulus Book, 2008).

Daniel J. Harrington, SJ, *Synoptic Gospels Set Free, The: Preaching without Anti-Judaism* (A Stimulus Book, 2009).

Richard C. Lux, *Jewish People, the Holy Land, and the State of Israel, The: A Catholic View* (A Stimulus Book, 2009).

.